The ONE YEAR, THIRTY MINUTE BUSINESS TRANSFORMATION

Fifty-two, thirty-minute exercises to make your organization healthier, your employees more engaged, your processes more efficient, and your bottom line fatter

MIKE CHIRVENO

Charleston, SC
www.PalmettoPublishing.com

The One Year, Thirty Minute Business Transformation
Copyright © 2021 by Mike Chirveno

First Edition

Paperback ISBN: 978-1-63837-630-9
eBook ISBN: 978-1-63837-631-6

DEDICATION

For Leslie,
My wife, best friend, and biggest supporter for more than forty years.
The willing sharer of every up and down that comes from being married
to a small business owner.

For Liz and Nick,
My kids, the two people who have brought more joy into
my life than any other two people in the world
(also great people and awesome parents).

For my Dad and Mom,
My dad was a small business owner his entire life. He taught me how to
work. This is the book I wish he could have had as a resource.
My mom cheers through every success and encourages
through every struggle I have as an entrepreneur.

TABLE OF CONTENTS

TABLE OF CONTENTS BY CATEGORY

FOREWORD

Mark G. Contreras
President and CEO, Connecticut Public Broadcasting, Inc.

Mike Chirveno has put together a literal handbook for a new business owner, longtime CEO, or executive of a large, multinational corporation. It is literally that versatile.

I had the great honor of working with Mike many years back and can see why he was the guy who the company could not do without!

The easily consumable and accessible content provide a great leadership map which can rejuvenate, improve, and inspire any organization—large or small—if the top leader follows it.

I'd highly recommend Mike's book as a necessary part of your leadership and management collection.

Jeff Hall
Former Newspaper Executive (VP, *Los Angeles Times*) and now
Digital Entrepreneur (Editor & CEO, TheLatest.com)

As a small-business owner, I know that the crush of daily demands has a way of pushing aside important things we all know we should do but just can't quite find time to do. Follow Mike Chirveno's thirty-minutes-a-week plan, and not only will your productivity go way up but almost all your ticking time bombs will be silenced. I've watched Mike do this in real life. It works.

Sharon Kinchsular
CEO, Greenwood Acres Company, Inc.

Growing up in a successful family business provided me with some tools and guidance to run a business myself for over twenty-five years now. Over those years, I attended college classes, went to seminars, watched webinars, and read multiple books, articles, magazines, and blogs all claiming they had all the answers to build and operate a successful business. Even though I was successful, I could see my business leveling off. It seemed mediocre.

When I started working with Mike Chirveno of ClearVision Consulting, he didn't claim to "know it all." He asked questions. He asked the right questions. He asked the questions I needed to answer for myself and my business.

Mike's *One-Year, Thirty-Minute Business Transformation* is genius. These weekly challenges are gifts he shares from his lifetime of experience. The consistent weekly exercises provide the foundation for the inevitable growth and success of your business. Mike's unique mentoring style, consistent support, and inspiration are unrivalled by even the most famous consulting gurus.

Brian O'Neil
Founder and CEO, Sales Empowerment Group Inc

As the founder and CEO of a company that's landed on the Inc 5000 (fastest growing US companies) for five years in a row, I know how hard it is to put out the daily fires in a business AND devote time to building a strong company with mature processes and a high-performing team.

That's why I'm happy to recommend Mike Chirveno's book, *The One-Year, Thirty-Minute Business Transformation*. It's a how-to book for all the activities that you must prioritize if you're going to build a solid company. And the format works—an exercise that pulls you out of your routine, takes thirty minutes a week, and comes with valuable online resources that makes the exercise easier to execute.

I've worked with Mike intermittently since founding Sales Empowerment Group and can tell you that he knows strategy and operations. This book takes that knowledge and breaks it down into bite-sized exercises that, if you'll do them, will transform your business.

Jose M Quintana
President, AdventGX, and Founder, The Innovation Underground

I have had the opportunity to work with Mike in a number of large and, many times, challenging projects. He is one of the most thorough, considerate, and hardworking individuals I know. His many accomplishments are a testament to his upmost integrity and business acumen, and this book reflects his passion for developing entrepreneurs.

If you own a business, you are an executive, or you aspire to be either, you will benefit from Mike's wisdom and insights. Not only you will learn and develop strategic thinking and advanced tactical skills, but you will also learn to develop the discipline needed to stay on top of the many aspects of leading an organization.

The One-Year, Thirty-Minute Business Transformation will become a "Required Reading" title in our entrepreneurial track at the Innovation Underground, and I'm certain both our team and our entrepreneurs will know greater success as a result of Mike's many thoughtful exercises.

Dr. Harry E. Stanley II
Business Owner

Struggles and challenges abound for the business owner, yet solutions are not so readily available. *The One-Year, Thirty-Minute Business Transformation* presents to the reader practical and actionable solutions while asking the serious questions to help the business owner stay focused on becoming more and more successful in day-to-day business and overall earnings. As business owners integrate the principles of *The One-Year, Thirty-Minute*

Business Transformation into their company, not only will their perceived value of the company be enhanced, but the economic value of their business will increase. *The One-Year, Thirty-Minute Business Transformation* gives you, the business owner, the tools to create the environment where your employees are encouraged to work independently while collaborating for the best outcomes of your business.

WHY THIS BOOK

Running a business is hard work. If you recently started, you might be facing unbelievable financial pressures. Maybe you pulled equity out of your house and maxed out your credit cards to monetize your dream. Now you're not sure if you can pay down that debt. If you've been at this awhile, you might be struggling with scaling your operations to meet demand. Maybe you keep hiring the wrong employees over and over and wonder if there's anyone who can work successfully inside your organization. Some of you might even be contemplating your exit. This book is for all of you.

The "tyranny of the urgent" clocks in every morning at your office, factory, restaurant, or practice. It never misses a day, and it always puts in a full day's work. It manifests itself in the underperforming vendor, the chronically late employee, the unreasonably demanding customer, and the broken-down delivery truck. It pulls you away from planning for future growth, working on organizational health, and developing your team.

I get it. And that's why I wrote this book. It's a bit of accountability sitting on your desk or eBook reader bidding you to step away from the tyranny of the urgent and spend thirty minutes a week deliberately making your organization healthier. It covers a lot of territory—problems that keep my business owner clients up at night. It's not high-minded theory. It's practical and actionable. But that doesn't mean it's mindless. It asks hard questions and provokes deep thought about your personal and professional growth, the growth of your team, the kind of organization you want to be (both internally and externally), and the tools and methodologies you're using to increase revenues, decrease costs, and fatten up the bottom line. It seeks to strike the right balance between being (who we are) and doing (how we act).

The chapters take five or six minutes to read. Then, there's an exercise. Some weeks, you can complete the entire exercise in thirty minutes. Other weeks, the thirty-minute exercise gets you ready for some homework you need to complete with your team.

- **It's multidisciplinary.** There are chapters on operations, finance, strategy, marketing, culture, personal growth, and more. I'm guessing most of them will apply in your organization, but some might not.

- **It's utilitarian.** The exercises walk you through exactly what you need to do to shore up that discipline in your organization.

- **It's transformative.** And really, that's the whole idea. The challenge baked into the *One-Year, Thirty-Minute Business Transformation* is to deliberately invest thirty minutes each week in your personal and professional growth, the growth of your people, and your organization's health to make it the company you've always dreamed of.

- **It's hard.** At least some of the weeks. You might be stepping into areas that aren't exactly in your wheelhouse. That's OK. You'll see that I admit to a few of those myself over the course of the book. To build the organization you've always dreamed of, every discipline needs to run the right way.

- **It's satisfying.** At the end of the fifty-two weeks, you'll be amazed at the transformation. You'll change, your team members will change, and your organization will change. And you'll be equipped with tools that will help you keep the organization healthy and growing for years to come.

- **You're not alone.** It's tough being the boss. Who do you talk to when you're not sure what to do? You might be a bit reluctant to talk to your team—they're looking to you for the answers, right? The book has a companion website, oneyearthirtyminute. com. You'll find additional resources there (explained in the next chapter), and you'll find an online community where you can ask questions and interact with others facing the same struggles.

Finally, I want to be a resource for you as you read through the book and afterward. Feel free to send questions, comments, and stories of transformation or struggle to mchirveno@clearvision.consulting.

Thanks for reading,
Mike Chirveno

HOW IT WORKS

The idea behind the One-Year, Thirty-Minute Business Transformation is to digest and implement one discipline each week for a year. Each chapter lays out the case for shoring up that discipline in your organization, then jumps into an exercise.

Some disciplines are people focused. Some are process focused. Some are customer facing. Some are employee facing. Some build hard skills. Some build soft skills. That's part of the challenge of being a business owner. You have to manage all the disciplines in the organization. For those disciplines that don't come naturally to you, you have to either learn them or surround yourself with people who excel in them.

You don't have to follow the exercises in order, but I have included a couple of things at the beginning of the book that, if left unattended, could cause you some heartburn. If there's an area that's causing you some sleepless nights now, find it in the table of contents and dig in.

Regardless of the order, here's what I suggest you do. Pick your chapter for the week and set aside uninterrupted time to read it carefully—don't let anything displace that appointment. Jot down anything that especially resonates with you. Some of the chapters suggest that you do the exercise alone. Some suggest you do the exercise with your team. For the team exercises, get the chapter contents to your team, so they can read it too. The exercises themselves are very straightforward. I'll walk you through the activities that will install that discipline in your organization. When you do an exercise, do it well. Be honest about the state of your organization. Ask hard questions. Don't make excuses. Implement completely. Don't skimp. Finish what you start.

For every chapter you can find resources at the book's companion website:
oneyearthirtyminute.com

You'll be able download forms, checklists, and supplemental materials. For team exercises, print copies of the forms for everyone involved. On the website you'll also find a place to share your One-Year, Thirty-Minute Business Transformation successes and struggles so that other business owners can benefit from your application of the information in the book. You'll have to register the first time you want to download info or join the discussion forum, but after that, all the content will be available. I want to hear from you too. You can email me at mchirveno@clearvision.consulting or message me on the book website.

I also think there's another very effective way to use the book. Buy a copy for each member of your leadership team, assign a chapter for the week, and use it as a discussion guide for the last thirty minutes of your weekly staff meeting. That will ensure that at least part of your week is devoted to working *on* the business and not just *in* it.

I'm committed to the success of business owners. This is one small contribution to that group of people that I admire greatly, people who have risked their personal treasure and banked on their God-given talent to build a better life for themselves and their family.

Good luck.

WEEK 1 :: PEOPLE :: CRITICAL PATH

"If he leaves, we're screwed."

I was part of that conversation. In fact, I was the "he" that was going to screw the company by my departure. I left a few months after the conversation. I'm not sure my former employer was "screwed," but when I resigned to start my consulting firm, my former employer was my first client and remained a client for the next seven years, accounting for a substantial part of my early consulting revenue. Through a series of circumstances that are too boring to recount here, I was the only person in the company that had a certain set of skills and information vital to my division's operational success. I had become part of the "Critical Path." The sequence of events needed to complete necessary tasks ran through me. I continued to complete those tasks but now was being paid as a consultant. The consulting work included training others to assume those duties and, in some cases, doing the work myself until the project was completed several years later.

As I began consulting, I found out that my situation in my former work life wasn't unique. There are lots of organizations that pivot on the knowledge and skills of one or two people. If one of those people gets hit by the proverbial bus, the organization suffers. The degree of suffering ranges from strongly inconvenienced to an inability to execute core value-creation activities, putting the company's existence in jeopardy.

This week's One-Year, Thirty-Minute Business Transformation is all about mitigating that risk–the risk of having all your operational "eggs in one basket."

Let's jump in.

- List three people whose absence, if they quit or were unable to work, would have significant operational impact on the business.

- For each of those people, identify the operational impact.

- On the graph below, plot the three people listed above based on their probability of leaving and the risk to the organization if they were to leave.

Presumably, if they made it into this exercise, they're going to land in the top half of the graph—i.e., their departure poses a risk to the organization. There are two situations that could make a departure particularly perilous:

- The employee is a critical path component in your company's delivery of products or services—i.e., if this employee were gone, your ability to generate revenue would be crippled. Depending on the length of the absence and the depth of this employee's involvement in critical path activities, this could put the entire enterprise at risk.

- The employee is a *single point of failure*—i.e., this employee is the only one who possesses a particular skill or a particular body of knowledge.

In either of these situations, the urgency for addressing a departure ratchets up significantly. For this exercise, the action items below assume the only variable is the employee's decision to stay or go. However, no person or company is exempt from unplanned events. That being the case, addressing these critical path employee issues is always urgent, even if the current employee is the most loyal and dependable in the organization.

For all the employees in this exercise (on both sides of the vertical axis), create the list below.

Employee	Most Critical Skill	Successor	Percent Ready
Mary	*Set up new vendor*	*Hannah*	*50*
Bob	*Enter new orders*	*Alice*	*20*
Mary	*Do Payroll*	*Steve*	*0*
Tim	*Update Admin Settings in CRM*	*Sarah*	*80*

It's possible, maybe even desirable, that a single employee will be listed more than once. If they have more than one critical path skill or single point of failure capability, you might want to split those skills and capabilities among multiple successors, thereby eliminating the single point of failure. List the successors and their percent of readiness.

Create an action plan for each successor to make them proficient in the critical path responsibilities. The plan should include

- knowledge to acquire,

- skills to master,

- experience to accumulate,

- and relationships necessary for execution and support.

Assign mentors for each activity (it's most likely the current employee but could be someone else), establish milestones, and set target completion dates. Check in with the mentors and successors to ensure that skills transfer is taking place.

If you have no one in the organization who could successfully execute the work of these critical path employees, start the process of recruiting, hiring, and onboarding suitable successors. In addition to your normal regimen of finding new employees with shared values and cultural fit, add the skills required for these tasks to the job requirements.

For those employees who plot to the right of the vertical axis (high risk to the organization and likely to leave), move quickly to mitigate the risk. What can you do to keep them in the organization until you've identified and trained a successor? If they are seeking greater challenges, can you assign them more interesting work while they identify and train their own successor? Given the critical nature of the activities it might be unlikely, but can you identify a vendor, contractor, or consultant who could step in if the employee's departure put the business at risk?

Finally, a bit of homework (definitely more than the thirty-minute exercise). Document the work of every critical path employee. Create documentation that details

- the "why" behind each of their activities,

- the people they interact with to accomplish the activities—vendors, customers, peers, supervisors, and subordinates,

- the systems they use (including usernames and passwords),

- the data they enter into those systems,

- any equipment they use to perform the work,

- who they call if that equipment malfunctions,

- any materials they use to perform the work,

- where they obtain replacement materials,

- any reports they use to inform their work,

- any notifications they make prior to, during, or after the work,

- and finally, complete, step-by-step instructions for the work itself.

If successors are not on board when you start this documentation process, you might have to do it yourself to make sure it's complete and easy to follow.

WEEK 2 :: BUSINESS CONTINUITY :: DATA

Business Continuity is the discipline that enables your organization to keep operating or quickly return to operations after an unexpected event, be it a natural disaster, manmade incident (robbery, arson, computer virus, malware, or ransomware), or even a catastrophic event caused by the actions of an employee or contractor.

The One-Year, Thirty-Minute Business Transformation will return to the topic of business continuity in a later chapter when we focus on operational items, but this week we're going to focus on one of the most valuable and irreplaceable assets in your organization—data.

You can buy more buildings, equipment, and vehicles and hire more people, but you can't buy more data. Data represents not just the historical performance of your company but, more importantly, the historical performance of your customers. And nothing is a better predictor of future behavior than past behavior. This data is a rich resource as you use it to increase efficiency and effectiveness internally. Externally, you can use it to segment customers and prospects and communicate with those distinct groups more clearly, even down to the individual level.

In the course of this exercise, I'll be mentioning companies and products to illustrate specific types of offerings and capabilities. Some of these I use, and some I don't. However, for all of these, I don't get any type of kickback or referral fee; they are for illustration only.

If you work in a larger organization with dedicated tech resources, you might be saying, "We've got this covered. We have a robust business continuity plan and we have people dedicated to taking care of this." Good enough, but skip to the bottom for some bonus content on the topic of stored data.

Let's get started.

Identify all of the data collected or stored by your organization. Here's a starter list:

- Financial data in your accounting system

- Sales data in your order entry system

- Customer and prospective customer data in your CRM system

- Operational data in your ERP system

- Inspection data in your manufacturing system

- Marketing performance

  - Website analytics

  - Response rates from advertising campaigns

  - Response rates from email campaigns

  - Social media posting with responses

- Shipping data in your logistics system

- Supply order history and vendor performance in your procurement system

- Employee data (including tax and benefit selection) in your HR system

- PLC programming for your manufacturing equipment

- Computer code for any software developed in-house

- Policy and operations documentation

- Promotional materials (templates, logos, sales collateral, etc.)

- Legal documents (incorporation papers, employment contracts, client contracts, etc.)

- Usernames and passwords for company accounts (website code, website hosting, accounting system, CRM system, social media accounts, online banking, eftps.gov, state DOR, state unemployment, etc.)

Enlist the help of others on your team to identify other data created or collected in your organization. Also, include the location of all important documents that only exist in a physical format (signed contracts, incorporation papers, etc.).

With your complete list in hand, identify where all of that data resides. For example:

Data	Location	Backup
QuickBooks Accounting System	Bob's PC	
Customers and Prospective Customers	salesforce.com	
Website	Mary's PC	
Sales collateral, logo	Tom's PC	
Incorporation papers	File cabinet in Amanda's office	

Some users might use have an application installed locally (QuickBooks, for example) but save the data file on the company's local server. Make note of both. In case of a failure, you'll need a copy of the application and a copy of the data.

Now circle back and note (in the third column) where that data is backed up (i.e., a complete, up-to-date, readily accessible copy). If you use cloud-based applications (Software as a Service or SAAS), for example, QuickBooks Online, salesforce.com, or zoho.com, your data and applications are already automatically available in case of a localized emergency. However, for all other data that resides on a local personal computer or local server inside your organization, note where the data is backed up. This is essential in case the piece of equipment that houses the data has a catastrophic failure or the entire location is destroyed or becomes inaccessible.

Consult with your in-house or contract technology expert to craft a data backup plan for each piece of data. For all locally hosted data, select a backup solution that, at least daily, makes a copy of all data and stores it on devices that are not in the same physical location as your organization. Here are a few options to consider:

- For mission-critical data residing on a local computer or server, you might consider an always-on, cloud-based backup like carbonite.com. Any time the device connects to the internet, the carbonite.com software will push an updated copy of the files you select to their cloud storage site, all happening without any intervention from the user.

- There are cloud-based storage solutions available from many excellent providers including Amazon (AWS) and Microsoft (Azure). These services can certainly be used for backups, but many companies have opted to store their live applications on these cloud-based services instead of on local servers. They are fast and reliable.

- Many companies have crafted hybrid private/public cloud solutions where data is stored both locally in a company-owned hosting facility and in a public cloud facility, sometimes simultaneously.

- For all paper-only documents, consider scanning them and keeping an electronic copy.

Remember, the goal here is business continuity. You want as little disruption as possible to your operation in the case of a natural or manmade disaster.

Once your backup plan is in place, check backups regularly and make sure you can restore production systems from the backed up data.

If your organization uses specialized hardware to create, capture, or utilize data (like barcode scanners or RFID scanners), you'll want to have spare hardware on-site to restore operations immediately.

For some organizations, being closed for even several hours can represent the loss of thousands of dollars in revenue. Having a strong business continuity plan, especially as it relates to data, can ensure that you can continue to provide services, create goods, bill customers, and pay employees without disruption.

Finally, on a semi-related note, create, if you don't have one, a document destruction policy. Data is incredibly valuable, but it also creates liability for your organization. A well-crafted, strictly enforced document destruction policy can mitigate that liability. After consulting with tax and legal professionals, let's say you decide you need to keep seven years of financial records, and, for marketing reasons, you need to keep ten years of customer order data. At that point, securely destroy all other data. If you have other data outside the scope of your document destruction policy, it can be subpoenaed during a legal proceeding, going back decades if you still have it available. However, if you can demonstrate that you have a document destruction policy, and you follow it by destroying all data outside the boundaries of the policy, you can eliminate that potential exposure. In addition, you don't have to pay to store it, and don't have to pay to retrieve it should it be requested.

WEEK 3 :: FINANCE :: FIXED COSTS VS. VARIABLE COSTS

I hesitated to do this one and especially hesitated to do it early in the One-Year, Thirty-Minute Business Transformation because it surfaces most frequently with solopreneurs (or those with just a handful of employees). Larger and older companies have already figured it out or else they wouldn't still be around. However, when I've seen it with past clients and corrected it, the results were so dramatic—it's often been the difference between staying in business and going out of business—I felt like I had to share it early on.

It's really just a math problem. Instead of explaining, let me illustrate and then give the steps for this week's exercise.

ABC Company charges $60/hour for their widget repairing service. ABC Company is very busy, doing all the widget repair they can handle. They are always booked a couple of weeks in advance. It might be because they are at the lower end of the widget repairing market. Their competitors charge $75–$80/hour for the same service. The owner of the company pays his widget repairing employees $35/hour (the market rate), leaving him what he calculates as a $25/hour margin. However, at the end of every month, he just has a few dollars in the bank–not even enough to cut himself a check that would equate to 40 hours per week at minimum wage. So what's the problem? It could very well be that the owner is failing to take into account fixed costs.

Fixed costs are those incurred by the business just by being open. They wouldn't change, even if the business serviced no customers or sold no products.

To illustrate with our fictitious organization, the owner of ABC Company pays these expenses each month:

Rent on the shop	$1000
Payments on two trucks	$600
Tools	$200
Truck Insurance	$300
Liability Insurance	$400
Utilities	$400
Cell phones	$400
Accounting service	$150
Internet service	$100
Health Insurance	$2500
Advertising	$500
Total	$6550

That's $6550 to keep the doors open and the lights on (so to speak). If the two widget repairers get 40 billable hours per week every week, they log 344 hours per month (40 hours per week * 4.3 weeks in a month * two repairers). To cover these fixed costs shaves $19.04 off each hour that ABC Company bills ($6550.00 / 344 hours = $19.04).

When the owner pays the widget repairers, variable costs kick in. Variable costs are those that are driven by volume of work or product produced–for instance, hourly wages, the cost of materials to build a product, shipping costs for a product, etc. In our example, the owner incurs variable costs of $35.00/hour in wages and an additional $2.67/hour to pay the employer share of Social Security and Medicare.

Here's what's left of the $60 the owner collects from customers:

$60.00 Customer rate
- 19.04 To cover overhead (fixed)
-35.00 To the widget repairer (variable)
 -2.67 To cover employer share of Social Security and Medicare (variable)
 $3.29 Remaining margin

So the $25.00 per hour margin the owner thought he was creating with his pricing and salary policy is really $3.29. Now it's apparent why his competitors are in the $75.00–$80.00/hour range for the same service. It's also apparent why he has no money left to pay himself at the end of the month.

You might be wondering if I'm exaggerating for purposes of this exercise. Unfortunately, the answer is no. I've worked with one client where the margin number was zero and another where the number was in the single digits.

Let's move on to this week's exercise.

- For the last three months, go through your checkbook or copy of QuickBooks (or whatever your bookkeeping methodology is) and list each fixed expense.

  Here's a starter list (it's by no means exhaustive). Go through your records and be thorough in finding every fixed expense.

  — Rent or loan repayment for your place of business

  — Vehicle payments or leases

  — Vehicle insurance

- Business insurance (property, liability, E&O, etc)

- Health insurance

- Professional services (accounting, legal, consulting)

- Technical services (website, internet, email, desktop support)

- Communication (landline, cell phone)

- Office supplies

- Advertising

- Administrative employees (those who would be paid even if no services or product were delivered)

- Property Taxes

Calculate the total fixed expenses for the 3-month period. Then, depending on your business type, use the steps below to account for fixed costs in your pricing model.

- For service businesses –

  - Keep the number from the previous step handy (total fixed costs). You'll need it for this exercise.

  - For the last three months, calculate the number of hours for which you can collect money from customers (billable hours).

  - Take the total fixed costs for the last 3 months and divide it by the total billable hours for the last 3 months. The quotient is the fixed cost that must be covered in each billable hour.

- Find the variable salary cost associated with one billable hour.

- Find other variable payrolls costs for one billable hour (typically Social Security, Medicare, vacation pay, sick pay).

- Find the rate the customer pays per hour.

- Total the fixed costs, variable salary cost, and other variable payroll costs and subtract the total from the rate the customer pays per hour. This is the net profit for each billable hour.

- If that number is less than the desired net profit for each billable hour, take one or both of these actions - increase the customer's per hour rate or find a way to decrease the fixed costs or variable costs until this number represents the amount of money you want to net for each hour of customer work.

• For businesses that sell products (but not in a retail setting) –

- Keep the number from the first step handy (total fixed costs). You'll need it for this exercise.

- Calculate the total retail value of all products sold in the last 3 months (for each item, quantity sold * retail price).

- Calculate the total cost of goods sold (COGS) for all products sold in the last 3 months (for each item, quantity sold * cost of goods sold). For purposes of this exercise, sales commission is included in this calculation.

- Add the total fixed costs and total cost of goods sold and subtract the total from the total retail value of all products sold. This is the net profit for the 3-month period.

- Divide the net profit by total retail sales. This is the profit margin (the percent of the retail dollar that you keep, before taxes, depreciation, etc).

- If the profit margin is less than the desired profit margin (the ideal profit margin will vary based on industry), take one or both of these actions - increase the cost of the product or find a way to decrease the fixed costs or cost of goods sold until this number represents the profit margin you want.

- If you sell multiple products at multiple price points, this gets more complicated. It's likely that more differentiated items justify higher prices and higher margins and can cover more fixed costs. It's also likely that some undifferentiated, commodity items will be subject to prevailing market prices, have razor thin margins and will, consequently, cover virtually no fixed costs. The only solution is to evaluate each SKU using the sale quantity, retail price, and cost of goods sold and calculate that product's ability to contribute to covering more fixed costs.

  - (quantity sold * retail price) − (quantity sold * cost of goods sold) = net profit for the SKU

- At that point, it's a SKU-by-SKU analysis to figure out which items justify a higher price point, can be manufactured or obtained at lower cost or both. Each item that fits that criterion can contribute more to cover the fixed costs. Competitor pricing also comes into play here. Finally, you might be able to justify a higher price point for creating a better customer experience (ease of ordering, ease of payment, quality of service after the sale) or for quicker delivery of your good or service.

- For retail businesses –

We're going to look at the retail sales in two different ways – fixed costs, variable costs and remaining profit, then we'll bring in the additional variable of hours.

  - Keep the number from the first step handy (total fixed costs). You'll need it for this exercise.

  - Calculate the total retail value of all products sold in the last 3 months.

  - Calculate the total cost of goods sold (COGS) for all products sold in the last 3 months. For purposes of this exercise, includes sales commission (if that's part of the compensation plan) and hourly pay for the retail staff (all payroll not included in the fixed costs number).

  - Add total fixed costs and total cost of goods sold and subtract the total from total retail sales. This is the net profit for the 3-month period.

  - Divide net profit by total retail sales. This is the profit margin (the percent of the retail dollar that you keep, before taxes, depreciation, etc.).

  - If the profit margin is less than the desired profit margin (the ideal profit margin will vary based on industry), take one or both of these actions - increase the cost of the product or find a way to decrease the fixed costs or cost of goods sold until this number represents the profit margin you want.

  - If you sell multiple products at multiple price points, this gets more complicated. It's likely that more differentiated items justify higher prices and higher margins and can cover more fixed costs. It's also likely that some undifferentiated, commodity items will be subject to prevailing market prices, have razor thin margins and will, consequently, cover virtually no fixed costs. The only solution is to evaluate each SKU using the sale quantity, retail price, and cost of goods sold and calculate that product's ability to contribute to covering more fixed costs.

- o (quantity sold * retail price) – (quantity sold * cost of goods sold) = net profit for the SKU

- At that point, it's a SKU-by-SKU analysis to figure out which items justify a higher price point, can be manufactured or obtained at lower cost or both. Each item that fits that criterion can contribute more to cover the fixed costs. Competitor pricing also comes into play here.

For the retail analysis, we want to slice and dice the same numbers one more way.

- Keep the number from the first step handy (total fixed costs). You'll need it for this exercise.

- Calculate the number of hours the retail or food establishment was open in the 3-month reporting period.

- Divide the total fixed costs by the total hours the retail location is open. This quotient is the average fixed costs to be covered for each hour open.

- Calculate the total hourly payroll (plus sales commission, if applicable) for the 3-month reporting period (all payroll not included in the Fixed Costs Worksheet).

- Divide total payroll by total hours open. The quotient is the average payroll per hour for each hour open.

- Calculate the total retail value of all products sold in the last 3 months.

- Divide total retail sales by total hours open. The quotient is the average sales for each hour open.

- Calculate the total cost of goods sold (COGS) for all products sold in the last 3 months. Don't include sales commission or hourly pay for the retail staff.

- Divide total cost of goods sold by total retail sales. The quotient is the percentage of each sales dollar that is used to cover the cost of goods sold.

- Create a table with these values –

  - Sales per hour
  - Sales per hour * percentage of each sales dollar used to cover cost of goods sold = COGS per hour
  - Payroll for each hour
  - Fixed costs for each hour
  - Calculate: Sales per hour – COGS per hour – payroll for each hour – fixed costs for each hour = net profit per hour

- This calculation is only slightly valuable since all hours in retail are not created equally. However, if your POS system can't produce the next piece of information, this will at least provide a bit of guidance.

- From your POS system, print a report showing sales by hour (i.e., 10 am – 11 am, 11 am to 12 pm, 12 pm to 1 pm, etc.). Ideally the system will allow you to run the report for a range of dates and calculate total sales by day of the week. For example, a 28-day range with all Sundays averaged together, all Mondays averaged together, etc. Using our example, you'll now have an entry that averages sales for 4 Mondays between 10 am and 11 am, and the same calculation for every other hour you're open. Then apply the items from the earlier bullet point, substituting the per hour sales from the POS report for the sales per hour. Calculate a new COGS for each hour by multiplying the sales per hour from the POS report * percent of each sales dollar used to cover COGS. From the POS report sales per hour, subtract the new COGS per hour, subtract the payroll for each hour, and fixed cost for each hour. Do this for each hour represented on the POS report. I realize you probably don't schedule the same number of people for each hour of the day. So, you can make this calculation more sophisticated by breaking down your hourly payroll number to a per employee rate, then calculating the number of employees typically scheduled for that particular hour.

- This exercise will help you identify hours that you shouldn't be open. Just remember, if you reduce the number of hours open, the fixed costs per hour number goes up.

Check these calculations frequently. As volume (more hours or more units) goes up, fixed costs per hour or per unit go down, until you increase volume enough that you must add fixed costs (hire another admin person, buy another truck, lease a bigger building). At that point, the math changes again.

I realize this week's exercise can get complicated very quickly. If the simple examples in this exercise aren't sophisticated enough for your business, consult your accounting or bookkeeping professional.

This exercise is incredibly important and could be the difference between staying around to serve customers for many years or being gone in just a few months.

WEEK 4 :: CULTURE :: CREATING A MENTOR MINDSET

Management guru Peter Drucker reminded us that, "Culture eats strategy for breakfast." Even the best strategies and tactics, when unleashed into a company with a toxic culture, are headed for certain death. All of you that have worked in a place with a toxic culture just offered up a hearty "Amen." We'll visit the topic of culture multiple times during the One-Year, Thirty-Minute Business Transformation, and this is one of those times. During the course of a consulting engagement, I'm occasionally asked if I have a list of cultural imperatives, that is, attitudes, approaches to work, and actions that should absolutely be baked into the DNA of the organization. I do, and one of those imperatives is a Mentor Mindset.

Without question, every leader in the organization should have the mentor mindset. But I'd advocate for screening for the mentor mindset when hiring even the most junior associate. The mentor mindset is that baked-in concern an employee has for making the people around them better. It's the opposite of the person who hoards what they know so they can leverage it for more power.

So here's this week's exercise. We're going to focus on two things: helping you practice the mentor mindset and prepping your staff to develop and practice the mentor mindset.

Helping you Practice the Mentor Mindset

Write one "why" you'd like everyone in the organization to understand. It might be why you forego cheaper raw materials for your product and insist on a specific high-quality input, why you insist that every customer be greeted in a specific way, or why you only promote from within.

For the "why" above, identify how understanding that "why" will change the way your team approaches their work. Will they be better able to explain to current and potential customers why your widget is better than your competitor's? Will they have a newfound appreciation of every customer who comes in the door? Will they better understand your goals for the organization? Will they gain insight into an existing process and now be able to make suggestions as to how to improve it since they understand the endgame?

Design a way to "mentor" by disseminating this information to your team. Is the best medium a companywide meeting? An email to everyone in the organization? A series of departmental meetings? A series of one-to-one meetings? A video posted on the company intranet? Whatever it is, make it happen by the end of this week. After you share the information, gather feedback. Was this new information? Did this correct an errant perception held by team members? How will this change their approach to their everyday work? Will this operationally change their work?

If this returned positive results, look for other "whys" you can share.

Here's a second exercise for you to try. When the next problem lands on your desk that only you can solve, identify someone else on your team that could solve it if they had more training, more experience, more perspective, or more information and go find them. Let them know that you don't want to be the only person in the organization that can solve this kind of problem, and you want them to carry this responsibility with you. Then, start at the beginning and walk them through the process of solving this problem. Show them how you gather information, explain your thought process in deducing the best course of action, show them the resources you use, show them how you communicate the solution, and anything else involved. I realize this process will take a lot longer than solving the problem yourself, but in this case the endgame isn't only quickly solving the problem, it's also building a stronger team.

The next time the same problem surfaces, pass it off to your team member and sit by them as they solve it. Over the course of several instances, let them take the lead. Soon, they will be proficient, and you've multiplied the problem-solving horsepower in your organization. And, who knows, they might even find a better way to solve the problem.

Helping your Team Practice the Mentor Mindset

When you model this behavior, it's a strong motivator for your staff do likewise, but here are a couple of deliberate ways you can encourage your staff to practice the mentor mindset.

- When you send a team member to a class or conference, ask them to prepare a written recap or short presentation of what they learned. Disseminate their recap or let them make their presentation to the rest of the team.

- Ask each of your direct reports to share a specific operational task (how they prepare for their staff meeting, how they order raw materials, how they prepare for a sales call, etc.) with one of their team members and have them ask that team member if they see any way to improve their work on that task.

- Ask each person on your team to document one of the tasks they do regularly. Collect all the documents and redistribute them to other team members. Have the team members critique the documents, looking for steps that are unclear or lack a "why." Send them back to the original author to be updated.

Doing every one of these exercises requires humility. Someone might find holes in your processes. Someone might identify a better way. But humility is a good thing and, in fact, ought to be one of the attitudes and approaches baked into our culture. This exercise is a good accelerator.

WEEK 5 :: MARKETING :: CLAIMING LISTINGS

In 2010, one of my new consulting clients was agonizing over some negative online reviews. He wanted to know how to delete them. I explained that deleting them was precisely the wrong thing to do. I went on to add that the best thing we could do is respond to them in the same online forum and explain in public—in front of that customer and everybody else—how we were going to address that customer's grievance. To say that the client wasn't on board with my recommendation would be a gross understatement. My engagement was terminated shortly after that conversation.

It's too bad because the client missed out on the benefit of the Service Recovery Paradox. The service recovery paradox states that customers can often be more loyal to an organization after they have experienced a service failure followed by a positive resolution than if the failure had never occurred in the first place. The research is mixed on the service recovery paradox, but in a world where almost every shopping experience starts online, the ability to demonstrate authenticity—"Yes, our company is staffed by humans who make mistakes, but when we do, we make every effort to make it right"—is a powerful way to start the conversation with potential new customers.

A 2018 study from Salesforce and Publicis.Sapient found that 87 percent of business-to-consumer shoppers begin product searches on digital channels, up from 71 percent the previous year. In two different studies, Blue Corona found that 71 percent of business-to-business researchers begin their research with a generic Google search, and Google found that 89 percent of business-to-business researchers use the internet during the business-to-business research process.

That bit of truth brings us to the topic of this week's One-Year, Thirty-Minute Business Transformation: Claiming Online Listings. There's a good chance that your business has a listing on Google, Bing, and Facebook even if you never created one. If I google my business (ClearVision Consulting), here's what the search results look like. Notice my website and LinkedIn page are on the left, in the search results list, and the Google Business listing is on the right.

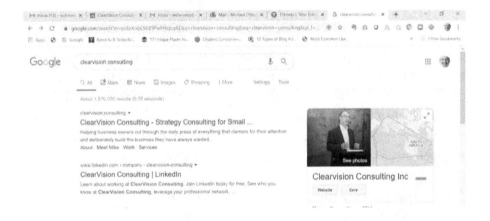

This week, I'm challenging you to claim all your online listings (if you haven't already), so you're in complete control of what people find when they begin to interact with you online.

The mechanics might be slightly different from platform to platform, but I'll be illustrating with a Google Business listing.

This is my business listing. You can tell it has been claimed by me because I have the option "Edit your business information." Google knows that I'm logged in to the Google account that manages the listing.

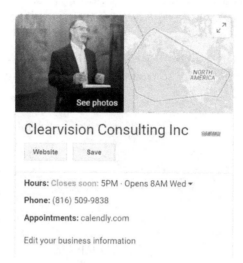

For an example, I've pulled the listing of a local business that has been claimed by the owner. My option at the bottom is to "Suggest an edit" to the page owner.

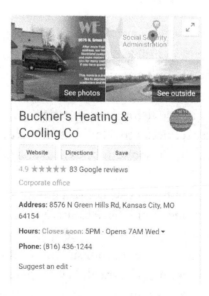

The last example is from an out-of-state business that has not been claimed by the owner. Notice the two options at the bottom—"Suggest an edit" and "Own this business?"; "Own this business?" indicates that the Google Business Listing is unclaimed. Any information on the page has been gleaned from other sources or from customers or others who have provided it.

To claim this listing, a responsible party (owner or manager) must click on the "Own this business?" link and complete a series of steps to verify that they are authorized to administer the listing. After those steps are complete, they can then build out the listing with the firm name, contact information, address, website, services provided, hours, pictures, and more. Most importantly, they can then respond to those who have left reviews.

I've provided links below to sites where you are likely to have a listing or might want to create a one. You'll have to survey the landscape and decide if your organization should be there. Some span a number of industries. Some are industry specific. Three or four sites in the list are used frequently by people in trades (plumbing, electrical, HVAC, etc.). Others are popular for food and services (like restaurants, bars, salons, and spas). Click on the links, search for your business, claim your listing (if it already exists), or create a listing. Make your listings consistent across all platforms—standardize name, address, contact info, website, hours, services, logos, and pictures.

Google My Business
https://www.google.com/business/

Facebook Business
https://www.facebook.com/help/257661877677443/

Yelp
https://biz.yelp.com/business_name_and_location

Yellow Pages
https://accounts.yellowpages.com/register

Yahoo
https://smallbusiness.yahoo.com/local

Bing
https://www.bingplaces.com/

Foursquare
https://foursquare.com/venue/claim

Home Advisor
https://www.homeadvisor.com/spa/zip

Angie's List
https://office.angieslist.com/app/join

Thumbtack
https://www.thumbtack.com/pro

Other than listing Facebook here, we've not discussed social networking. That's another topic for another day. This exercise is all about being accurately represented in search. The more relevant and accurate listings there are for your organization, the more likely you are to be found. When those listings accurately represent who you are, the more likely people who want your product or service are likely to engage with you.

For those of you who are now super intrigued by this exercise, here's a list from HubSpot of the fifty best local business directories.

https://blog.hubspot.com/blog/tabid/6307/bid/10322/the-ultimate-list-50-local-business-directories.aspx

Happy claiming.

WEEK 6 :: PEOPLE :: COGNITIVE DIVERSITY

Diversity has been in our corporate lexicon for about thirty-five years.

> "In 1987, the Secretary of Labor, William Brock, commissioned a study of economic and demographic trends by the Hudson Institute. This study resulted in the text titled, 'Workforce 2000—Work and Workers in the Twenty-First Century.' Workforce 2000 highlighted demographic factors that would impact the labor market in the United States. In a nutshell, the book argued that the US would only continue to grow increasingly diverse and suggested that diversifying the workforce was an economic imperative if companies wanted to stay competitive and attract talented employees."
>
> —Shakti Diversity and Equity Training

Clearly, the authors of the study were on to something—the workforce is now more diverse than it was then and is getting more diverse every year. Social scientists project that there will be no majority ethnicity in the US by 2045 (https://www.brookings.edu/blog/the-avenue/2018/03/14/the-us-will-become-minority-white-in-2045-census-projects/). And there's certainly been no shortage of corporate diversity programs in the ensuing years.

So with this influx of diverse workers and the, most likely, millions of hours of diversity training, are we successfully leveraging the cultural and intellectual horsepower of today's diverse workforce?

That brings us to this week's One-Year, Thirty-Minute Business Transformation. We've done some things right in our diversity initiatives—we've clearly recognized the changing face of our workforce, we've been proactive in recruiting, and we've sounded the trumpet for inclusivity. But I'm not convinced that we've unleashed the most important superpower of a diverse workforce: Cognitive Diversity, that is, the value of those who think differently. Silicon Valley has an incredible concentration of engineers and rightly so. But now the companies that employ those engineers are hiring art, music, and philosophy majors. https://www.edsurge.com/news/2019-02-25-dear-liberal-arts-major-stem-companies-need-your-skills-to-grow Why? Because they think differently.

In many ways, an education is a framework for solving problems. When you hire an engineer and especially a herd of engineers from the same school, you get people who solve problems the same way: like an engineer. So no matter how many of them you have, they bring an engineer's approach to tackling a problem. Aim a musician at the same problem, and you're likely to see a much different approach.

Many times, our diversity initiatives have focused on observable differences—gender, ethnicity, and age—but have neglected a big difference that makes our organization better: a different way of thinking. If a company who hired only white, male Harvard MBAs tried to become more diverse by hiring a black female Harvard MBA, an Asian male Harvard MBA, and an Indian female Harvard MBA, they've shortchanged themselves. I'm not discounting the innate differences in each of us nor the differences that come from different upbringings, different cultures, or different life experiences, but if we want a big upgrade to the intellectual horsepower of our organization, we need people who think differently. We cheat the organization when we solve for only half of the equation.

One more observation before the steps for this week's exercise. Almost without exception, when I work with a business owner, especially a newer owner, the first few hires are clones of the owner. It's no wonder, for we like people who are like us. If we're going to trust our business to another person, we want someone we trust implicitly, and someone like us seems like a safe choice. I get it, but we're missing out on the benefit of cognitive diversity in our newly formed business.

So what do we do to leverage cognitive diversity in our business?

1. *If you've never defined a set of core values, start here.* We absolutely want people who think differently in our organization, but those people must share a common set of core values. Whenever I'm doing this exercise with a client, I never allow them to choose values like honesty, integrity, or hardworking—no business is out there looking for employees who are dishonest, lack ethical moorings, and are lazy. Honesty, integrity, and hardworking are price-of-admission values. You don't even get to play in the game without them. Instead, discover those things that are integral to the way you do business. Maybe it's a love for small-business owners. Maybe it's love for a craft like woodworking, car mechanics, or logistics. Maybe it's an unswerving devotion to customer service. Maybe it's a commitment to lifelong learning. Find those things to which you would be committed even if your business evaporated into thin air.

2. *Identify barriers to cognitive diversity in existing operations*

    a. Is dissenting opinion welcome in the organization? Is it possible that you once had cognitive diversity but drove it away by shaming or discounting dissenters?

    b. Are you hiring over and over from the same talent pool (in terms of education and experience)?

    c. Are you hiring only those people who are clones of owners or other employees?

    d. Is engaging in acceptable risk encouraged? Are failures OK assuming the project sponsor mitigated foreseeable pitfalls?

    e. Are employees encouraged to weigh in on parts of the business that are not strictly in their purview?

3. *Build cognitive diversity through engagement with existing employees and through new hires*

    a. In problem-solving meetings, after you've reached a conclusion, ask one or two people to argue against the conclusion you just reached.

    b. In problem-solving meetings, break the attendees into two groups and ask each group to take fifteen minutes and create a solution. Let both groups present their solutions and argue the merits. Adopt one, create a mashup of both, or go back to the drawing board.

    c. Assign a small group of employees to an existing company initiative and identify why the company is doing it all wrong (to be an assigned devil's advocate).

    d. Allow employees to work on a project of their own choosing (this is how Google got Gmail and 3M got Post-It Notes).

    e. In recruiting, identify positions where you could hire for alignment with core values, introduce cognitive diversity, and train for the specific job—can you teach a willing art major how to analyze shipping data or train new call center reps?

    f. Identify cognitive biases that keep you from hiring a perfect candidate for a job because they are not "like you."

Clearly, this can require quite a bit of uncomfortable self-reflection (more than some of the other exercises in *The One-Year, Thirty-Minute Business Transformation*), but it can generate some very powerful problem-solving horsepower in your organization.

WEEK 7 :: GROWTH :: REFRAMING

This week's One-Year, Thirty-Minute Business Transformation makes us look at our organization through a different lens.

Many of you have probably seen this. Connect the four dots with two straight lines. The lines must touch but not cross.

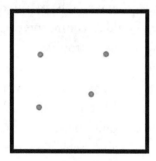

If you're stuck, it's because you tried to keep the straight lines inside the box. That wasn't one of the requirements.

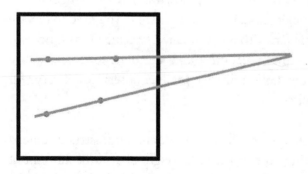

When we ponder growing our organization, we typically plan incremental growth that we could handle within the framework we already employ—for example, if we grew x percent, we could ask the office staff to work some overtime, or we could hire another technician. I'm all in favor of incremental growth and that type of growth is always welcome. However, for this week's One-Year, Thirty-Minute Business Transformation, I want you to think differently. I want you to ask the question, "What would it take for us to do 10X (ten times) the business we are doing now?" The genesis for this week's exercise (but not the exercise itself) comes from Larry Page at Google who asks his team to look for 10X opportunities.

So here's this week's exercise.

Identify the changes to your lead generation activities that would be required to generate 10X the number of leads you have now. Would it require entering new markets? A larger sales staff? Additional advertising platforms?

To get to 10X sales, what would it take to increase your closing rate? If you close 10 percent of all sales presentations, what would it take to close 20 percent? What additional information would the customer need? A more meaningful connection to your company's message (your "why")? Access to existing client testimonials? A better understanding of your company's value proposition?

To increase velocity of service delivery after a closed sale, what changes would you need to make to customer onboarding activities? Do you need to replace your paper-based order system with an automated system? Do you need to ramp up your after-sale communication so that customer expectations are clear, and they know exactly how and when product or service delivery will begin and how it will look?

To handle 10X the business, how will your production infrastructure need to change? Will the existing process bear the weight of 10X the amount of business or does a new production infrastructure need to be built from the ground up with the ability to scale? Do you have suppliers that can deliver 10X raw materials on time and with the required quality, or do you need to add suppliers or seek a new supplier? Do you need to find subcontractors that can supplement in-house production? Can they do it with the same quality and meet your time constraints? Can you invoice and collect from 10X the number of customers, or do you need to provide new billing or financing options that will keep your 10X cash flow healthy?

To follow up with 10X customers, do you need a more robust CRM system that can manage increased customer communication, customize communication, and deliver valuable information after the sale? Can the system deliver ongoing useful information that will position your organization for more sales in the future?

Clearly, this brief exercise can't touch on every element that you might need to 10X your business, but that's not the purpose. The purpose is to help you think differently about business growth. Most of the time, we approach business growth like we approach speeding up on a bicycle: to increase velocity, we intensify existing activity. We do more of the same thing we've always done, that is, we pedal faster and longer. This will work for a while, but at some point, we max out the load-carrying capacity and speed of the bicycle. To make our business grow, we need to swap the bicycle for a motorcycle or a delivery van. More speed, more capacity. We must change platforms.

The value of this week's exercise will come when you identify the pieces of your organization that won't scale. When you find irreparable platform deficiencies where no amount of "pedaling" will fix them, and they must be replaced. When you find people-constrained activities that must be replaced with repeatable processes.

All of us would like 10X growth, but doing this exercise will position your organization for 2X, 4X, or 5X growth on the way there, and you'll be building an organization that is more platform-driven, process-driven and policy-driven, and that's good for everyone in the organization.

WEEK 8 :: VALUE CREATION :: VENDORS

Vendors can be a critical path component in your value-creation chain, or they can be a completely undifferentiated source for something as mundane as trash can liners. Regardless of where they fall on that spectrum, they're going to get some attention in this week's One-Year, Thirty-Minute Business Transformation.

The vendors you use for commodity purchases probably don't significantly impact your ability to build sustained competitive advantage. However, even these vendors can cause some grief if they're late with orders, have inexplicable pricing or returns policies, or are chronically terrible at resolving screwups. With the wide variety of vendors available for these commodity purchases, spend a little time finding one who anticipates well, is conscientious, and is easy to do business with. Enough said.

On the other end of the spectrum are those vendors who are deeply ingrained in your value-creation chain. These vendors are partners in every sense of the word. We often call this special vendor relationship *outsourcing*. At the outset, outsourcing was typically something that large businesses did to save money. Call centers were moved halfway around the world to take advantage of a skilled workforce that provided services for a fraction of what a domestic workforce was paid. Factory workers building TVs, shoes, and hundreds of other items allowed manufacturers to keep costs low, pass along savings to customers, and boost profits. Outsourcing has changed dramatically over the years. Now, businesses large and small look to outsource vendors to

- obtain specialized services they don't possess in-house,

- get services that the outsource provider does better than they do it in-house,

- easily scale up and down to meet fluctuating demand,

- focus their attention on core value-creation activities while outsource providers take care of tasks that don't add value to products or services,

- resell additional products or services that they do not produce in-house,

- and provide services more economically than they can in-house.

So, let's jump into this week's One-Year, Thirty-Minute Business Transformation.

For which disciplines in your organization might outsourcing make sense?
Early discussions on outsourcing targets focused on core vs. context activities:

- Core being those activities where the company was creating value for customers—the activities that made the company unique.

- Context being those activities that provided the company no additional brownie points with customers even if they are done perfectly.

The conventional wisdom was to outsource context and keep core in-house. Current thinking is a bit different. Skilled outsource providers now deliver services that empower employees to do better work and enable the company to deliver better products and services to their customers.

Here are some options for outsourced services. Some might be on your radar now and some you might not have explored yet. Read through the list and see if any of these might improve company operations, improve customer experience, mitigate risk, or boost the bottom line.

- *Payroll.* Managing payroll related documents, collecting hours worked, calculating paychecks, cutting checks, making direct deposits, providing year-end tax documents, providing management reporting, and providing an online payroll portal for employee self-service. Beyond these core services, many providers deliver extra unique services like 401k's.

- *Human Resources.* Providing training, consulting, and resources for hiring, development, and termination. Providing templates for important documents like noncompete agreements and nondisclosure agreements. Providing insight on the broad variety of pre- and postemployment assessments available. Ensuring client compliance with everchanging federal and state employment laws.

- *Bookkeeping.* Entry of financial data, accounts payable, accounts receivable, general ledger, and invoicing. Providing management reporting and filing.

- *Accounting.* Providing management reporting, advice on cash management, use of debt and equity financing, tax preparation and minimization of tax liability, collections, shareholder relations, business growth, business valuation, and more.

- *IT Infrastructure.* Building and maintaining wired and wireless internal networks; internet access; deployment and maintenance of desktop, portable, and mobile hardware; data security; backup and disaster recovery; email; desktop productivity software, collaboration software, and integration with third-party software providers (Customer Relationship Management (CRM),

Enterprise Resource Planning (ERP), Supply Chain Management (SCM)).

- *Big Data/Analytics.* Using data from transactional systems (CRM, Accounting, ERP, etc.) and sometimes supplementing with data from external sources; performing analysis and providing actionable insights on trends, patterns, and associations previously undetected.

- *Outbound Logistics.* Managing all facets of storage and distribution after goods are produced. The provider often picks up items directly from the end of the assembly process and, with information from the client's order entry system, either warehouses, forwards to another location for additional processing, or ships the item leveraging a larger and oftentimes more sophisticated distribution system.

- *Marketing.* Help with branding, identifying target markets, messaging, and choice of mediums. Some firms provide advertising design and procurement, website design and development, Search Engine Optimization (SEO), paid search, social media management and advertising, print collateral, email marketing, and CRM systems.

- *Lead Generation.* Identification of prospective clients, initial contact, lead development, and appointment setting. Firms employ a range of methodologies including email marketing, telemarketing, and LinkedIn prospecting.

- *Consultants.* With a broad range of disciplines available, consultants provide short-term, mid-term, or long-term engagements in areas like strategic planning, execution, operations, customer experience, process improvement, leadership, management development, technology, marketing, or project management. Utilizing a consultant allows an organization to "rent" expertise not present in the company or to extend the reach of expertise already present in the company by adding additional resources.

Evaluating Existing Vendors

For vendors already in the fold, use these criteria:

- Do they communicate regularly, clearly, and completely about the status of new initiatives, ongoing projects, and problems?

- Do they provide clear, concise, and easy to consume information about their performance?

- Are problems resolved quickly and completely?

- Do you have easy access to key personnel in the vendor organization so that you can get questions answered and quickly ramp up new initiatives as needed?

- Does the vendor organization regularly contribute new ideas or suggest new services that will increase revenue, improve customer experience, streamline operations, strengthen technical expertise, improve marketing reach, or develop employees in the client organization?

- Does the vendor provide special product or service knowledge that stops the client organization from deploying their product incorrectly or enables the client organization to use their product in new or different ways to better service the client's customers?

- Does the vendor suggest better or alternate products or methodologies that solve a problem more effectively for the client's customers and feel free to intervene in suggesting the alternate products?

- Does the vendor willingly forego business (i.e., not sell a product) if it's in the best interest of the client or the client's customers?

Evaluating New Vendors

Technical Competency. I'd suggest developing a list of questions by vendor type that you submit to every prospective vendor so that you can compare apples to apples when you get the written responses back. There's not time here to do a list for every type of vendor, but let me illustrate with the beginning of a list for an IT services vendor.

- What levels of services are available, and what are the response times for each level?

- What percentage of time do you meet the required response times?

- Tell me about the technical qualifications of the staff at each support level: certifications, experience?

- Do you have preferred vendors for each product type? What type of compensation do you get from that vendor for using their products? How can I be assured that I'm getting in best-in-class solutions if you use only products from vendors who commission you to use their product?

Company Fit. Not all of these fit in every circumstance, but these are some of the questions I use when evaluating a new outsource vendor regardless of the service I'm seeking.

- How long has your company been around?

- What is the staff size?

- What is the experience of the staff? (in years and professional background)

- What is the turnover rate for employees? (I want to know if employees are happy working there.)

- How much time do employees spend in training every year? (I want to know if the company has a learning orientation.)

- Is any part of your operation outsourced? (I want to know what level of control they have over the people who will be servicing my account.)

- What is the financial condition of the company? (I want to know if they'll be around next year.)

- Where is your company located? (Time zones can be a challenge.)

- Who runs your company and what are their credentials and experience?

- Have you worked in this industry before? (I never let this disqualify someone. It just tells me if there are certain industry-specific things I'll need to educate them on.)

- How much have you spent on R&D in the last twelve months? (I want to know if the company is growing and innovating.)

- Are you insured?

- How do you deal with ongoing regulatory compliance issues?

- Can I get a list of references? (Call them.)

- How soon can we get started?

- Can I see an onboarding packet or something equivalent?

- Do you have other clients our size?

- Who is your toughest competitor?

Run through these lists to identify new outsourcing opportunities, evaluate existing outsource relationships, and be better prepared for entering into new relationships.

Vendors and outsource partners can be powerful allies in building value. Choosing and managing them can quickly improve customer experience, operations, and profitability.

WEEK 9 :: STRATEGIC PLANNING :: STAYING EVEN, GETTING AHEAD

This week, *The One-Year, Thirty-Minute Business Transformation* visits my favorite topic—Strategic Planning. Unfortunately, many owners and managers forego strategic planning because they believe their business isn't big enough, they don't know how to do it, or the item never bubbles to the top of their to-do list.

I'm afraid strategic planning is bit misunderstood (like the fact that tomatoes are fruit). It's not mystical, and it's not just for big, publicly traded corporations. It's for every organization, public or private, big or small, for-profit or not-for-profit. At its core, strategic planning is *truthful evaluation, thoughtful options, and deliberate actions to move your organization from the current state to the desired state.*

We'll revisit strategic planning a few times during the One-Year, Thirty-Minute Business Transformation, providing exercises that will make you think about where you are, where you'd like to be, and how you're going to get from the former to the latter. In each exercise, we'll keep the scope very narrow, singling out a single topic that's usually part of a more overarching strategic planning process.

Let's jump in.

Organizations operate in rapidly changing environments. Today's success doesn't guarantee tomorrow's success. An organization with expert capabilities today can come up short tomorrow.

Look at the matrix below.

Let's walk through the four quadrants, starting with the bottom left. Your organization has a set of current capabilities. With those capabilities, you access a certain set of opportunities. That's your business as it is today.

Let's move to the bottom right. Since the environment in which we work changes rapidly, in the future, you'll need to add capabilities to access the very same opportunities. Let me quickly illustrate. It wasn't that many years ago that all you needed to work on a car was a timing light, a dwell meter, and a toolbox full of wrenches and screwdrivers. Now what do you need to work on a car? You need sophisticated diagnostic equipment that plugs into the car's onboard computer, so the car can tell you what's wrong with itself. Then, you need the toolbox full of wrenches and screwdrivers. So to deliver the same result—a car that runs correctly—you need new capabilities (and in this case new equipment). Just staying even requires new resources and skills.

Let's move to the top left. There you might find the ability to access new opportunities using your existing capabilities or resources. Many years ago, when I worked for the *Kansas City Star* newspaper, we capitalized on an existing resource by combing through the thousands of pictures in our archives that had been collected over several decades. With them, we produced and sold beautiful coffee table books highlighting things as diverse as the history of the city and a collection of random, unique doors in the city. You might have a similar ability.

Finally, there's the upper right box—greenfield opportunities—opportunities that have never been accessed by your organization or even better, opportunities that have never been accessed by any organization. What new opportunities could you access if you added new capabilities? Think back a few years to Microsoft's entry into gaming. Up until that time they developed software for personal computers and servers—operating systems, software development tools, and office productivity tools. By adding new capabilities (gaming hardware and gaming software development), they were able to access new opportunities: a new gaming platform (Xbox) with a killer complementary product (Halo).

Let's walk through the steps of this week's exercise.

What will it take to stay even, to continue delivering the products or services you deliver now to the same set of customers?

- What new knowledge or skills will your existing workforce need to add?

- What new employees with what new skills or abilities will you need to hire?

- What equipment will you need to upgrade or acquire?

- What changes to products, services, or customer experience will existing customers expect just to feel like the value proposition is the same as it has been historically?

- Are you at a point where "staying even" means abandoning a current product and adopting a successor product? Think VCR to DVD or video rental to streaming.

- What services or features have been introduced into your industry that have now become "baseline"? The absence of them seems like failure, but the presence of them earns you no brownie points—think Wi-Fi at a hotel or online services at a bank. These must be present as well.

- What new distribution channels or communication channels must be added? Think interacting with new and potential customers on social media or enabling buyers to order and receive products digitally.

What else can you do with existing capabilities and resources?

- Can you expand to previously untapped geographies?

- Can you access previously untapped markets? For example, producing a consumer version of an existing industrial product.

- Can you deliver a new service with existing capabilities or a new product with existing resources?

- If you have excess capacity, can you act as a subcontractor for another company in the same industry? It could even be a competitor.

- Can you leverage your capabilities to manage a function for another company? If your bandwidth is wide enough, and your expertise is deep enough, you could establish a revenue-generating business unit that provides that service. It could be a great way to diversify and provide growth opportunities for talented staff members. And that unit could provide the service back to your parent company.

What greenfield opportunities could you access if you added new capabilities?

- Are there adjacent areas to your existing business? For example, adding commercial roofing to residential roofing. You can capitalize on an existing supplier network and most likely leverage some of your existing expertise.

- If your company has its own version of 20 percent time, can you bankroll the work of an existing employee, spin off their creation, and become an active shareholder who provides not only capital but coaching?

- Can you acquire another company with complementary product or service offerings? You can merge and leverage already existing administrative resources or leave it as a wholly owned subsidiary.

- Can you engineer a strategic partnership with a vendor or a trusted partner in an adjacent industry? Together, can you create a product or service that neither one of you could create on your own?

Gather some trusted lieutenants and maybe an outsider or two (your CPA or a consultant) and work through these bullet points. Keep a list of the tasks or ideas that bubble up.

Pay the most immediate attention to the "staying even" list. Begin assembling human resources and reworking processes, products, and services. Check competitors, listen to customers, use data, and marry all of those with what you know about moving the needle in your industry. Sometimes customers don't know what they want next until they see it.

Engage your team in identifying promising new opportunities that are accessible with existing capabilities. Craft plans to evaluate the opportunities, narrow the field, make a choice, and begin work on the options with the best return on investment.

Finally, challenge your team to identify greenfield opportunities. Pursue those with the biggest potential upside.

WEEK 10 :: METRICS :: BALANCED SCORECARD

Every time you check in at the doctor's office, they take your temperature, pulse rate, respiration rate, and blood pressure. There are thousands of medical measurements that assess a variety of health factors, so why those four? With decades, even centuries, of experience, medical professionals have deduced that these four measurements are indicative of baseline health. In fact, they're called "vital signs" because if each of these numbers isn't within an acceptable range, the patient's life might be in jeopardy.

In this week's One-Year, Thirty-Minute Business Transformation, we want to talk about the business version of vital signs. They're a bit more complicated than medical vital signs because they're most likely different from business to business, but they're no less important.

My tool of choice for business vital signs is a Balanced Scorecard. A balanced scorecard is typically six to twelve metrics that span four categories—Financial, Operational, Learning and Growth, and Customers. Once the metrics are identified, they're collected regularly (monthly, weekly, daily, or even hourly), compiled, and reported to everyone in the organization. Everyone then knows if the organization is "winning" and, when it's not, knows that the efforts of everyone in the organization need to be trained on getting the flagging metrics back in line.

Let's jump into this week's exercise.

Sociologist William Bruce Cameron observed that, "not everything that counts can be counted and not everything that can be counted counts." This catchy little quote sums up the most important task in this week's exercise—identifying the right metrics. Tracking, measuring, and reporting something that isn't truly indicative of organizational health might do more harm than good because you'll be constantly correcting something that doesn't really push your organization closer to executing its mission or reaching its vision.

Gather your most trusted team members and start working through the four categories, one at a time—financial, operational, learning and growth, and customers—and begin making a list of what you *could* measure. Within reason, make the list as long as you want.

One quick note on identifying metrics that are more unstructured. Some hard metrics will jump out at you immediately—top line revenue, Return on Invested Capital, gross margin, number of defects per thousand widgets produced, etc.—but at this point, you might not be measuring things like employee engagement, employee learning, or customer satisfaction. That's OK. Don't worry about the how. You just want to identify the things that are truly indicative of organizational health.

Now, with your four category lists in hand, work through each list one item at a time, asking:

- If we fail at this, do we go out of business?

- If we succeed at this, does it build sustained competitive advantage?

- Is this integral to us executing our mission?

- Is this integral to us reaching our vision?

- Does this have an added benefit of making the organization itself stronger?

You can even make a form:

Metric	If we fail at this, do we go out of business?	If we succeed at this, does it build sustained competitive advantage?	Is this integral to executing our mission?	Is this integral to us reaching our vision?	Does this have the added benefit of making the organization itself stronger?
Metric 1	X		X		
Metric 2	X	X	X	X	X

After this initial culling, each category list should be quite a bit shorter. Now, for each list, rank the items from most important to least important. With the ranked list, if the list has more than three items, can you remove item four or any items below it and not touch any item that was tagged "If we fail at this, do we go out of business"? Incidentally, if you have a "go out of business" item ranked four or below, you might want to reassess your list.

At this point, you want to have no more than three items in each category. If you have four on one of your lists, it's not a terrible problem. But four in each category would get you to sixteen, and that's too many.

If you need to do a bit more culling to get the total of all four lists to six to twelve, have at it. Weigh all list items against the others and remove the ones that don't make the cut. The shorter the list, the better. If you can reliably measure organizational health with five total items, go for it. That's less to track and less for your team to focus on to see if they are "winning."

The next couple of steps are mechanical. How will you collect the data, and how will you disseminate it? Some of the scoring will most likely come off the Income Statement, Balance Sheet or a production report. Earlier in the exercise, I asked you to only identify metrics that you wanted to track and not worry about whether or not you had a methodology for collecting it. That's because the item might have not made the cut. However, if it's on the final list, you need to create the methodology for scoring the metric. How will you measure employee engagement? Turnover? Online survey of all employees? Exit interviews? Productivity? That's a quick example. Each metric measurement that doesn't exist will require its own meaningful methodology.

You can use a variety of methodologies for disseminating the results. You can send companywide emails, use a companywide communication tool like Slack, put up dashboards on TVs scattered through the office, warehouse, or factory, convene a Friday afternoon meeting and present the scores. The options are only bound by your creativity. Early on, there's a big education responsibility. As the balanced scorecard is rolled out, everyone in the organization needs to understand why each item made the cut, why it's vital to the business, how it's scored, and what activities move the needle.

Finally, we reach the second-most important part of this exercise. If selecting the metrics is the most important part, doing something about them is a close second. Most of you are probably familiar with the term "diving for the ball." In football or basketball, if an offensive player fumbles the ball (football) or loses the ball on a dribble or wayward pass (basketball), everyone on the team "dives for the ball." At that point, it doesn't matter how the ball got loose. The only thing that's important is getting it back. That's very similar to what should happen with the balanced scorecard. When new numbers are reported and any of the results are flagging, it's time for everyone on the team to step up, even if it's not strictly their job. If one of your metrics is sales, and sales are down, everyone in the organization should ask, "What can I do to increase sales?" Working outside your discipline can often yield incredible ideas that are new to the organization. It kills ego in the organization because team members in the struggling discipline get help from those who are not experts in that field. It increases focus, teamwork, and cross-discipline understanding. After the flagging result is corrected, you can go back and figure out how the problem occurred—and you should—not to punish the guilty party, but to fix the process so it doesn't happen again.

When the next set of numbers are posted, team members can celebrate shared victories together or reconvene for additional focus on still-flagging numbers.

OK. An apology is in order. This will clearly take more than thirty minutes, but the results will be worth it.

WEEK 11 :: VALUE CREATION :: EXPERIENTIAL VALUE

If you or I were swinging through a fast food drive-through and placed an order for one of their value meals, and the voice on the speaker announced they'd be collecting twenty-five dollars at the window, we'd put a quick halt to that order. Why? Is it because we're opposed to paying twenty-five dollars for a meal? Probably not. We've most likely paid that much or more for a meal at our favorite restaurant. We're just opposed to paying twenty-five dollars for *that* meal because the value proposition doesn't work for us. Twenty-five dollars should buy us a better dining experience than a burger wrapped in paper, fries in a tiny cardboard box, and a soft drink in a paper cup. Experiential Value is the gap between what the customer pays for our product or service and the utility and enjoyment the customer experiences from the purchase. We want the gap between what the customer pays and pleasure they derive from the purchase to be as far apart as possible. We've already visited value creation in the short history of the One-Year, Thirty-Minute Business Transformation, but we're going to touch on it again—this time, exploring steps to maximize the customer's experiential value.

We're pretty good at calculating Economic Value because the math is very easy:

What the customer pays
- What it costs to produce the good or service
————————————————————————————
Economic Value

The math for calculating Experiential Value is a bit more squishy because it involves the sometimes subjective value that customers assign to their experience with our product or service.

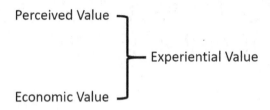

How do we do build the experiential value? I think some of the best advice comes from an extremely practical book by Rich Karlgaard, *The Soft Edge*. In the chapter "Taste," he reminds us that we can interact with every purchase on three levels. Unfortunately, we rarely do. Let's talk about them.

Function — Form — Feeling

Function is the most rudimentary level. I purchase an oil change for my car, and I get an oil change—new filter, new oil. I get the service, and I pay the bill. Very transactional. Even if the product or service is a bit more sophisticated, it can still be only transactional. It could be a new computer, a medical procedure, or meal at a sit-down restaurant. As long as there's an equitable trade, we're satisfied with the transaction. Clearly if we get less than what we expected, we're going to feel jilted. We might ask to speak to a manager, leave a one-star online review, or, most likely, never return. But if the transaction works, we might come back. Not a disappointment but nothing special either.

Form is the next level of engagement. Was the item we purchased not only functional but beautiful or especially easy to use? I not only got a good diagnosis and treatment in the medical office, but beyond that, the waiting room was bright and cheerful, check-in was easy, and the magazines were from this decade. This level of engagement made the transaction easy and even pleasurable. Next time I need this product or service, I'm likely to return because both the product and the delivery were great.

Feeling, the last level of engagement, is difficult to find, but it cements customers to the company that provides it, and it even forges personal bonds between the customer and representative of the company. It imbues the transaction with meaning. The customer connects with the company over shared values, and the customer feels validated for choosing this company to provide the product or service. Simon Sinek might call this "finding customers that share your 'why,'" or Seth Godin might call it "finding your tribe." Whatever it is, it's a connection that turns customers into brand ambassadors. It's the company you tell your friends about. It might be the great meal delivered by a friendly, attentive server. It might be the doctor who delivered bad news but sat there unhurried in the treatment room until your last question was answered, even though you knew other patients were waiting. When customers connect on function, form, and feeling, the bond with a business is strong, loyalty is high, and it can drive premium pricing because the relationship has moved beyond transactional to the customer's desire to repeat that feeling. Any employee can deliver feeling with the right amount of coaching and the right support from the organization.

Why have I gone to great length discussing function, form, and feeling before kicking off this week's exercise? Because expanding the distance between what the customer pays and the enjoyment and utility they experience is hard to do, but the payoff is big, and the payoff is long. Here's another important thing to know about strong experiential value: it buys you a mulligan or two. If you've succeeded at connecting on feeling and subsequently, on a future interaction, fail on function or form, you're most likely going to get a chance to make it right, maybe multiple chances. Still, as in all business transactions, you ought to work like crazy to earn it every time you get the chance.

So let's jump into this week's exercise.

This is getting mentioned almost every week—gather your most trusted team members and work through these topics. Doing this with your team allows you to mentor and to see the strengths of various team members as they embrace the subject matter. It might also allow you to identify topics for employee development. Keep notes, create action items, and assign them to specific people to carry them out. In a couple of weeks, reconvene and check on progress.

Function

- How does your product (list the factors) deliver the basic functionality that your customers seek? For example:

  - It's a fairly priced, quickly served, tasty fast food meal.

  - It washes dishes using an appropriate amount of water and detergent in an acceptable amount of time.

  - We show up on time, and the garage door works when we're done.

- For the question above, which of these rudimentary tasks could we screw up the easiest, causing us to fail at the most basic level? For example:

  - We frequently schedule jobs too close together, causing us to miss appointment times.

  - The final price regularly comes in above the estimate.

  - We frequently run out of items on the menu.

- What can we do to hedge against failure in delivering these baseline products or services?

Form

- How can we improve the delivery experience?

  - Can we communicate better before, during, and after the sale?

  - How can we improve customer onboarding so that expectations are clear and realistic?

  - Can we make the product or packaging more attractive?

  - Can we improve usability, making the product easier to access?

  - Can we make the invoicing and payment process easier or faster?

Feeling

- Can we make customer feel smarter, better, or more noble by purchasing and using the product or service?

  - Can we demonstrate that the value proposition is demonstrably better than the value proposition for those who purchased competing products? If your warranty is twice as long as your competitor's, let the customer know they are insulated from problems twice as long as everyone else who bought a competing product. They made a smart purchase.

  - Can we give them access to a customer service experience that will get them immediate help if they need it?

- Can we show that they supported a cause (think Tom's Shoes who donates a pair of shoes to charity for every pair of shoes purchased by a customer) or a group of people (a locally owned family business or a group of now fairly compensated foreign farm workers) with their purchase?

- Can we identify our connection (a real connection not a contrived one) with a group of people to whom they already feel connected (such as veterans, environmental advocates, gun owners, small-business owners, or artisan food makers)?

One quick note about all of this. Customers and potential customers can smell a phony a million miles away. Function, form, and feeling have to be delivered by an organization that sincerely embraces a desire for an excellent product or service, delivered in a winsome way by people who sincerely care about and want to connect with their customers. Anything less, and none of this works.

For those who do it well, delivering on function, form, and feeling will generate increased loyalty and create enthusiastic brand ambassadors for your organization.

WEEK 12 :: OPERATIONS :: GENCHI GENBUTSU

In the last few One-Year, Thirty-Minute Business Transformation exercises, I've encouraged you to assemble some trusted team members to complete the exercise. This one is a solo effort. In fact, going solo is at the crux of this exercise.

The inspiration for this week's exercise comes from the *Toyota Production System (TPS)*. TPS is the poster child for operational excellence. One of the tenets of TPS is *Genchi Genbutsu*. It literally means "real location, real thing." You might have heard the usual shorthand for this tenet, "*go and see.*"

Why is it mandatory for an owner, manager, or supervisor to "go and see"? Because some things can only be understood by being experienced. Many years ago, I managed a call center. There was a central group of thirty-five phone agents that handled most incoming customer inquiries and another thirty-five agents in five ancillary groups that handled more specialized tasks. For the three years I ran the call center, almost every Wednesday morning (our busiest weekday), I took calls with the operators for three or four hours. I sat in the same cubicles, used the same chairs, talked on the same telecom equipment, typed on the same hardware, used the same software, and talked to the same customers. It was the mother of all educations. And the benefits were enormous. I got bigtime "street cred" with the customer service reps. I knew what equipment wasn't working well. I knew what functioned well with the software and what needed to be changed in the next version. I knew what customers were happy about and what they were frustrated about. My BS meter was finely tuned when I talked to my staff.

I was able to argue persuasively when I talked to my boss about resources. I would have had none of this had I not "gone and seen."

Over my fourteen years as a consultant, I've checked in resort guests, unloaded trucks, stocked shelves, talked to client customers about software problems, responded to client customers on social media, and more. Why? Because I was working with clients to design processes they could roll out to teams, and those processes had to be right. They had to work for employees and customers, and they had to be able to scale. When I rolled out those processes to additional teams at the client site, they had been battle-tested, and I had the scars to prove it. Afterward, when I was back in the boardroom with owners and CEOs, I was able to report on my work with confidence because I knew that what the client teams and I had created together was bulletproof. When I was advising the client to invest additional resources, I had both empirical and anecdotal evidence that the resources were needed.

The exercise for this week is very simple. What is that operational problem that won't go away or that process that just seems clunky? The best way to solve it is "go and see." You might be spending time with your sales team calling prospective clients. You might be on the factory floor examining people, production steps, or equipment. You might be hanging out in the accounting department looking at the way you process vendor invoices. You might be evaluating vendor performance. Whatever it is, approach it with the least amount of prejudice possible. Ask a lot of questions and listen intently to the answers.

Here are some questions to answer as you flesh out the operational problem and begin to design the solution. As brilliant automotive inventor and engineer Charles Kettering said, "A problem well stated is a problem half-solved."

- How did we first become aware of this problem? From a customer? From an employee?

- How can I get the "deepest drink" from this on-ground experience?

- How long will it take to get an accurate picture of the circumstances that surround this problem?

- How are employees impacted?

- How are customers impacted?

- How is revenue impacted?

- How are expenses impacted?

- Are we more concerned about "fixing the problem" than "fixing the blame," and have we communicated that clearly?

- How much of the problem is self-inflicted?

- Is it attributable to poor product quality or poor service delivery upstream?

- How quickly can we rectify the product or service problem?

- Can we identify other upstream causes of the problem?

- Can we identify other downstream consequences of the problem?

- Is it traceable back to a vendor?

- If so, do we have an alternate source that will solve the problem?

- Can this problem be solved with money?

- Can this problem be solved with a process change?

- Is the problem caused by a management failure—lack of resources, poor working conditions, failure to deal with a problem employee, unrealistic expectations, lack of training?

- Is this problem tied to a "sacred cow" that needs to be sacrificed?

- Are we hesitating to "pull the plug" because of sunk cost?

- Have I asked the people most intimately involved how to solve the problem?

- If not, why not?

- Can we enlist someone from another discipline to look at the problem, leveraging expertise from an "outsider"?

- Is this a value-creation activity that should remain in-house, or is it a candidate for outsourcing, especially if the outsource provider could do it better and eliminate the problem?

- After we have a rudimentary understanding of the circumstances surrounding this problem and begin to address it, how can we stay connected to it to make sure the corrective actions are working?

"Go and see" isn't effective just for solving operational problems; it's also a reliable way to design processes for new initiatives.

WEEK 13 :: LEADERSHIP :: PERSONAL GROWTH

There will always be dozens of things in your business clamoring for your attention—some small and some coronavirus-size. These urgent matters scream for attention and keep screaming until they are resolved. Unfortunately, most of the time, fixing them probably won't have a huge effect on the long-term success of your organization.

It takes discipline to step away from screaming urgent matters, even for a few minutes each week, and focus on organizational health and future growth. But there's one even more important factor in the health of your organization, and it won't even make a peep when it's neglected.

An organization won't ever be healthier than the leaders in that organization. Consequently, every leader in the organization needs to carve out time for personal growth. This week's exercise isn't thirty minutes' worth of personal growth; it's thirty minutes of planning a personal growth strategy that will permeate several areas of your life.

I think we mistakenly segregate pieces of our lives—secular and sacred, personal and professional, academic and practical. In the next few paragraphs, I'm going to advocate for a wide range of activities that will build a more unified, holistic life. A life that allows you to be the same person at home, at work, at play, and at worship. This approach will make you a more effective leader in your organization. You'll be a "whole person," fully engaged no matter where you are.

Take thirty minutes and decide which of these activities are most needed, most interesting, and most motivating and get them on your schedule. There will be immediate impact on your personal life, your family, and your business.

Strengthen your spiritual life

Animals live by instinct. They can't make moral and ethical choices. That's the sole territory of us as human beings. The moorings for those moral and ethical choices come from our spiritual life. I find my moorings in my Christian faith. Find yours. Here are some recommended resources:

- The Old Testament book of Ecclesiastes. The richest and wisest Old Testament king of Israel discusses the meaning of life

- *Searching for God Knows What* by Donald Miller

- *The Reason for God* by Tim Keller

Get healthier

We desperately need not just the physical benefits of exercise but the mental and emotional benefits. People who exercise regularly see reduced anxiety, reduced depression, improved cognitive function, and increased self-esteem. Exercise is only half the equation. Getting healthy also means monitoring what we're eating and drinking. There are no diet recommendations coming, but moderation is a good discipline in every area of life.

- Join your local gym. It's not only a great way to keep in shape but also a great way to support a local business.

- There are several new, interesting options for in-home workouts that incorporate online classes with in-home equipment.

- At the local park, take a walk or bike ride with your family.

- Involve the whole family in healthy meal planning.

- Shop together and cook together.

Stretch your brain

After a long day at work, it's tempting to spend the evening binge-watching a favorite series. That can happen in moderation, but I'd encourage you to spend some time getting smarter. Be deliberate about growing as a spouse, parent, and business leader.

- Read a book. I have some specific recommendations depending on where you are in your professional life.

  - Early in your career: *So Good They Can't Ignore You* by Cal Newport, *Range* by David Epstein

  - Later in your career: *Late Bloomers* by Rich Karlgaard, *Range* by David Epstein

  - Managing and developing your team: *Drive* by Dan Pink, *First Break All the Rules* by Marcus Buckingham

  - Impacting others: *Getting Naked* by Patrick Lencioni, *Trillion Dollar Coach* by Eric Schmidt

  - Thinking strategically about your business: *Good to Great* by Jim Collins, *Great by Choice* by Jim Collins, *How Google Works* by Eric Schmidt

  - Value Creation: *Think Beyond Value* by David Flint, *Competing Against Luck* by Clayton Christensen

- Marketing: *Building a Story Brand* by Donald Miller, *This is Marketing* by Seth Godin, *113 Million Markets of One* by Chris Norton

- Personal Productivity: *Deep Work* by Cal Newport, *The One Thing* by Gary Keller

- Take an online course. Learn how to program from codeacademy. com. Even if you have no interest in computer programming, the discipline of writing code teaches thoroughness and helps you think you through things in order. Or maybe exercising the right brain is in order. Take an art class or learn to play an instrument. YouTube is loaded with free resources.

Get a mentor/be a mentor
Every one of us needs someone pouring into us, and we need to be pouring into someone else. Look for potential mentors/mentees at work, your place of worship, or in a networking group. You can meet virtually or in person.

- Clarify personal and professional goals and make a plan to take the next step.

- Ask for help identifying blind spots.

- Be humble and share failures and mistakes.

Create margin to do great work
Carve out time to create valuable work products. Put it on your schedule. Don't let anything displace it. Consider new markets. Create new products. Hone the messaging on your website. Redesign your employee onboarding material. Redesign your customer onboarding material. Write a new class for employee development. Plan and outline a year's worth of blog posts.

- Block out big chunks of time (three to four hours) and don't allow any distractions.

- Spend time alone to create. There is science behind the great ideas we have when we're showering or mowing the yard. So to kick off some heavy-duty creative time, take a walk (no phone) or do some yard work.

- Aim for "flow," work that is interesting, engaging, and not too hard yet not too easy.

Don't set new goals. Instead, create a personal and professional strategic plan

Goals are great, but strategic plans are better because they have baked inside them the steps to get from where you are to where you want to be.

- Start with your desired exit (which might be a long way away) and work backward.

- Set incremental goals and identify the skills and experiences needed to reach them.

- Plan specific steps to acquire the skills and experiences you need to reach the first incremental goal.

Deepen relationships

All of us need meaningful relationships. Spend time with family and friends. Your business rises and falls on your leadership. Keep learning and keep growing.

"Give me six hours to chop down a tree, and I will spend the first four sharpening the ax."

—Abraham Lincoln

WEEK 14 :: STRATEGIC PLANNING :: AGILITY

I probably used the phrase "pivot and survive" more in 2020 than in any other period of my life. It was the order of the day as we navigated the coronavirus and all the changes that accompanied it. However, the absence of the coronavirus (and the absence of the next ten crises after the coronavirus) won't remove the need for us to successfully pivot and survive. This week's One-Year, Thirty-Minute Business Transformation is about Agility, the skill that allows you to successfully pivot and survive.

Typically our ability to be agile has been the difference between

- capitalizing on an emerging opportunity or missing out,

- quickly fixing an emergency operational problem or allowing it to linger a little too long,

- and/or shifting staffing or methodology to meet a deadline or waiting too long to make a change and missing the target completion date.

We might have been disappointed when we missed out on a couple of bucks or took some heat for missing a target, but we learned during the pandemic that the stakes could be considerably higher. Our inability to be agile could have jeopardized the future of our organization.

Agility isn't a thirty-minute exercise; it's an organizational discipline that gets stronger the more it is practiced. So the goal of this week's One-Year,

Thirty-Minute Business Transformation is to lay the groundwork for agility. We want to introduce some attitudes, vocabulary, and tools that you can introduce during team meetings and begin to utilize as you read and react to a business environment that is changing rapidly every day.

Face Reality. Jack Welch admonished us to "face reality as it is, not as it was or as you wish it to be." Get out the Income Statement, the list of receivables (by client) and payables (by vendor), and the Balance Sheet. No rose-colored glasses allowed. Make sure everyone around the table understands what they're seeing. Call out the things that are good and the things that are troublesome. Talk frankly about people, products, service delivery, and the future (as you know it today). Even the most sacred of the sacred cows should be evaluated.

Question Assumptions. All plans are built on assumptions—the number of customers who will walk in the front door, the products they will buy, the amount of money they will spend, that employees will show up for work, that credit will be available, etc. Are all those assumptions valid today? Create a new set of assumptions that you're going to use going forward.

Embrace Ambiguity. Change is a constant. The world is not picking on you personally nor on your business. Take in new information, test it (to see if it's true), then add it to your knowledge base. The best NFL running backs read and react. They see the holes opened by their offensive line (planned), and they see holes opened by defensive missteps (part of the changing environment) and run through them. In times of rapid change in the business environment, chart your course similarly.

Innovate Effectively. Use changing circumstances to supercharge innovation. We mistakenly think that the best innovation comes from freewheeling, wide-open, unlimited-budget brainstorming. Nothing could be further from the truth. The best innovation comes from very narrow constraints—How can we solve this problem with $1,000? What changes to the customer onboarding process can we decide on before we leave this room and implement before the end of the week?

Leverage Existing Resources. What products or services could we deconstruct and sell separately? What products or services could we deconstruct and recombine to make new products more suited to the current environment? Who has existing expertise that we are not utilizing now? What underutilized inventory could we liquidate to invest in operations or in new inventory that we could turn easily in our new environment? If we are fiscally solid right now, what loans could we buy out and save money in the long run? What agreements for needed products or services could we strike with vendors who desperately need cash flow?

Think Broadly and Deeply. Agility requires the most effective cross-discipline work your organization has ever done. To paraphrase David Epstein in *Range*, mental meandering is a competitive advantage. If you and your team were afloat in a sinking ship, everyone would be encouraged to bail water, not just those with a job description that included water bailing. So it should be in an agile organization. Team members should be encouraged to contribute across departmental boundaries. Good solutions are the goal, and egoless team collaboration is the methodology.

Make Small Targeted Investments. As new ideas surface, test them as cheaply as possible. Do things by hand at first until you know they merit having a process built around them. Go to market with a "minimum viable product." Fail fast, iterate, and try again. When you've finally, by iteration, hammered out a workable new product, service, or process, begin to economically build systems around it. As Jim Collins reminded us, "Fire bullets, then cannonballs."

Remove Cumbersome Bureaucracy. Organizations that are agile embrace entrepreneurial-style decision-making, pushing down decision-making to the lowest level possible. When speed is a competitive advantage (and most of the time it is), layers of red tape hinder progress. Leaders should quickly "clear the path" for those creating or recreating a new product, service, or process.

This week, deliberately introduce one or more of these agility-enabling tools into interactions with your team and encourage adoption. It can be one-on-one or in a group setting. Over the course of the next few weeks, keep introducing more of these tools.

WEEK 15 :: TECHNOLOGY :: EVALUATING PRODUCTIVITY

When I was listing the topics I wanted to cover in the One-Year, Thirty-Minute Business Transformation, Evaluating Technology Productivity was an early entry. I knew it was important and that it represented a struggle for business owners and managers. But the fact that it defies succinct diagnosis, lacks easy measurements, and has a "more than I'm comfortable with" amount of subjectivity pushed it this far into the schedule.

Certainly, the return on investment (ROI) of some technology is apparent. A customer-facing e-commerce site generates sales numbers that can be compared to the cost of running the site. The return on other tech investments is tougher to quantify. If you invest $20,000 in security and never have a customer data breach or never have a bout with ransomware, what's the return? It's hard to quantify the value of an event that never happens. If you invest $2,000 per month for a Customer Relationship Management (CRM) subscription for your entire customer-facing team, and the sales funnel is always full and customer problems never fall through the cracks, can you calculate how much of that is directly attributable to the CRM?

That being said, I'm a big believer in tech-enabled enterprises. I like measuring metrics for web, email, and social performance. I like tracking every touch with current and potential customers using a CRM. I like Enterprise Resource Planning (ERP) systems that integrate supply chain, human resources, transformation activities, and finance. I like collaboration tools that supercharge organizational learning. But the question remains, "Am I getting my money's worth?"

For those pieces of tech where the ROI is a bit squishier, I want to offer some tools for subjectively measuring tech effectiveness. Like many of the One-Year, Thirty-Minute Business Transformations, this would be best handled with your leadership team. Get them together and work through these questions, one tech tool or application at a time. It will work for both in-house and hosted applications.

Process Support. Could you do your work without the tech tool or software? Is it integral for scheduling, manufacturing, distribution, communication, or personal productivity? Does it make the work easier or faster? Are there shortcomings in the tool that frequently surface that make the work more difficult, make it take longer, or stop the work altogether?

Integration. Is the tech tool or software easily integrated with other pieces of software or hardware in the organization? Can you easily pass data back and forth between other tech tools in the organization?

Reliability. Is the tech tool or software always on? Is it frequently down or unavailable because of maintenance?

Ease of Use. Do most employees use the tech tool or software as you intended, or do they look for ways to avoid it? Do they opt for a manual workaround or use a personal tech tool instead? Do they complain about functionality (such as too many screens or too many clicks required to get to the information needed), the user interface, or lack of available reporting? Is information readily available when it's needed to resolve an operational issue or solve a customer problem? Do they complain about lack of vendor support?

Support. When the tech tool or software is experiencing a problem, does the vendor respond and repair the problem in a reasonable amount of time?

When the tool is scheduled for an upgrade, do the upgrades work without causing additional problems? Do you have consistent communication with the vendor so that you are aware of new capabilities, new products, subsequent revenue or savings opportunities, or improvements to the employee or customer experience?

Ease of Configuration. Does the tech tool or software make it easy to add a new product, change pricing, add a discount, change a process, or affect other operational changes? Do you have to call the vendor for changes you feel like you should be able to make yourself?

Security. Is the data stored inside the tech tool or software secure? Is the data and application infrastructure "hardened" against physical attacks, cyberattacks, and internal breaches by employees or vendors? Is there sufficient user-level security (only allowing users access to information they need for their work)?

Reporting. Does the tech tool or software provide readily accessible, accurate, and actionable information? Is information presented in sufficient granularity so that you can evaluate the performance of individual employees, customers, products, and services? Is the information accessible to every person that needs it?

Money. Does the tech tool or software allow you to drive additional revenue? Can customers schedule online, purchase online, add complementary products, see additional available services, or easily pay online? Does the tech tool or software save money for the organization by automating tasks, improving accuracy, or reducing defects?

If the tech tools or software in your organization don't measure up in the light of these criteria, it might be time for a change. Depending on the complexity and the level of integration, it might be as easy as stopping one subscription and starting another, or it could be an extremely complicated and long undertaking. Don't hesitate to get help if it's needed.

WEEK 16 :: CULTURE :: LEARNING ORIENTATION

None of us, no matter how skilled, can afford to stay the way we are. Our industry, employees, and customers change, and so must we. Even if the founding generation and current generations have done everything right in steering the organization to its current state, their work may not be applicable in the future. We must be lifelong learners.

Lifelong learning embraces the idea that we never will "arrive." Our business acumen, industry awareness, and personal skills can always improve. Gary Keller in his book *The One Thing* reminded us that we must commit to running our organizations "the best it can be done" not "the best we can do it." The "best we can do it" imposes the limitation of our current capacity and intellect. "The best it can be done" introduces the possibility that we can seek out new information and new skills that will make us better managers and leaders.

Not only must we as leaders be committed to lifelong learning, but we must build lifelong learning into the culture of our organization. Every team member must see personal and professional growth happening in those who lead the organization and must have opportunity, tools, and accountability to affect their own personal and professional growth.

Let's jump into this week's One-Year, Thirty-Minute Business Transformation. The goal this week is twofold. Use your thirty minutes to

- think through everyday tasks and recreate them as learning opportunities,

- and/or create tools and time for team members to deliberately grow personally and professionally.

Reframe Tasks. Stephen Covey reminded us to "begin with the end in mind." When navigating the mundane, fixing the urgent problem, or capitalizing on the immediate opportunity, work to identify and verbalize how that task pushes the organization toward overarching initiatives (strategic plan, new sales campaign, etc.). To illustrate, let's say one of our new long-term strategic objectives is to, by the end of the year, decrease product delivery time from four days to two days for 90 percent of all orders. Today's issue has to do with billing for an order from a brand-new customer. The customer wants to set up an account and be billed since they plan on doing more business with us in the future. However, upon submission of their billing information, we find some problems with their credit information and even find some unfavorable credit reporting in an industry reference publication.

We could work with the employee who reported the problem to get this new customer set up and billed (and we should), but it would be best to reframe this problem and examine it in the light of our strategic initiative. In order to get this new customer their order in two days (in fulfillment of our long-term initiative), do we need to make changes to our order process to identify problems like this earlier? Do we need to look for a way to programmatically check credit reporting when the order is submitted online? Do we need to change the sales process, so prospective clients with credit problems are excluded from the sales pipeline? Reframing problems—and slightly expanding their scope if necessary—attaches larger meaning to the problem and makes solving the problem tactical instead of operational, moving the organization closer to reaching its long-term initiatives and making everyone involved in the process better equipped for the future.

Put Employees First. When urgent problems surface, they are, most of the time, screaming to be solved right now. Our natural reaction is to solve them ourselves or get them quickly to the person who can solve them best and fastest. What about using urgent problems as a training opportunity? Take an employee who has the requisite knowledge to solve the problem but has never had the opportunity and walk them through it as you solve it. Or pair them with the staff expert in solving the problem and let them walk through it together. It might take slightly longer, but afterward you'll have a deeper bench. If today's urgent matter is an emerging opportunity, show the employee how you step through an evaluation to make the determination whether to pursue it further. This helps the employee to see how you evaluate opportunities in the light of the organization's mission, vision, values, and current long-term initiatives.

Go from the Outside In. In the press to make problems go away or make the internal processes behind our mundane tasks easier for us, we occasionally make decisions that generate unintended consequences. Many times, the recipient of those consequences is not us but our customers. By making life easier for us, we make it harder for them. Amazon famously sits an empty chair in every meeting. That chair represents the customer. It's a physical reminder to make decisions that get the customer better products and services, make transactions more frictionless, and deliver more value for their money. When problems surface, start with the customer perspective and work inward, navigating through the company's internal processes. Solve the problem so the customer wins. Team members engaged in this exercise build a stronger customer orientation.

Embrace Cross-Discipline Problem-Solving. In his book *Range*, David Epstein tells the story of two labs working on the same problem at the same time (proteins they wanted to measure would get stuck to a filter, which made them hard to analyze). One lab, staffed by only E. Coli experts, took weeks to solve the problem, experimenting with multiple methodologies. The other lab, staffed by scientists with chemistry, physics, biology, and genetics backgrounds, plus medical students, figured out the problem in their initial meeting. Were the staff members in the latter lab that much smarter than those in the former lab? Unlikely. Those in the latter lab had the advantage of a much broader base of knowledge and a larger pool of diverse experiences. To build lifelong learning in an organization, leverage the knowledge of employees with diverse skills and experiences. Turn the finance people loose on an operational problem. Invite the IT people to weigh in on a sales problem. Create cross-discipline meetings and encourage collaboration to solve problems. Let team members experience the problem-solving methodologies of people from other departments.

Be Deliberate. Finally, provide resources for growth. Start a business book club inside the organization led by the CEO or GM. Meet once a month during lunch to discuss a chapter. Encourage employees to attend classes and webinars. Ask them to report back to the organization on ideas they found especially helpful. Encourage cross-discipline learning. Pay for a salesperson to take a Python or accounting class. Formally recognize those who are learning and growing both personally and professionally.

The goal is to bake the actions that promote lifelong learning into the culture.

WEEK 17 :: PEOPLE :: ONBOARDING

The struggle for talent is real. Hiring managers kiss lots of frogs on their way to finding a well-hidden prince or princess. And when they find a stellar employee, the organization is challenged quickly to find the best way to engage them in meaningful work and give them opportunities to lead and grow. And, maybe more importantly, those employees must work seamlessly with a new team that must quickly produce results where the whole is greater than the sum of the parts.

Onboarding is the key activity to accelerate the integration and productivity of newly hired employees. Successful onboarding starts even before the hire, continues through the offer and acceptance, and wraps up a few months into employment.

For purposes of this week's One-Year, Thirty-Minute Business Transformation, we're going to assume that during the recruiting and hiring process, you made sure the new employee is a good fit with the company's culture and embraces the company's core values. If that is not the case, the onboarding activities are all paddling upstream and will ultimately end in the employee's soon departure.

Let's jump into this week's exercise. I'm going to list several things newly hired employees need to understand and experience. During the thirty-minute exercise, I'm going to ask you to open a Word document or pull out a notepad and, item by item, identify opportunities in your current onboarding process where new hires can get that information and experience. Then, I want you to customize those items, so they work for your organization.

Finally, I want you to think about who could most effectively deliver the information and experiences—it might be you.

- **Pair the new team member with someone who models the culture fully and can explain it in detail.** You already checked for culture fit during the hiring process, but onboarding is the chance to flesh that out. Remember, culture must be caught *and* taught. I suggest using an employee commitment document that spells out the employee's commitment to the organization, team members, customers, and personal growth. If you want a sample employee commitment, email me.

- **Explain the company's value-creation activities.** How does the company create a product or service that customers are willing to pay for? What are the key components of the process? Where do the key activities take place? What benefits do customers derive from the product or service? What tangible or intangible advantage do customers receive that make them willing to pay more money than what it costs the company to create the product or service?

- **Explain how the new team member's job fits in that value-creation process.** How does their work create a better customer experience, make the product of higher quality, or drive costs down? How can they increase economic value creation for the company or experiential value creation for the customer? Implicit in this conversation is an explanation of the team member's new job responsibilities.

- **Attach purpose to the work.** Companies must make money to survive, but they must not exist solely to make money. It's comparable to saying that humans exist solely to breathe. We must breathe to exist, but we all aspire to more than just breathing. Help the new team member attach greater meaning to the work of the organization. Maybe you give families more leisure time by making everyday responsibilities faster and easier. Maybe you provide a venue where guests can make vacation memories that will last for a lifetime.

- **Understand the new team member's personal and professional goals.** The most effective way to manage employee development is to align the employee's interests with the interests of the organization. To make that happen, you must understand the employee's goals and aspirations and craft growth plans where those goals intersect with the organization's future needs. Every employee wants to be good at their job. Help them get there *and* simultaneously realize their own personal growth goals.

- **Help them integrate into the organization.** Marcus Buckingham's important work documented in *First Break All the Rules* details the importance of relationships in the workplace. Happy employees have a "best friend" at work and have someone speaking into their personal and professional development. The nuances of relationships in the workplace are impossible to address in a short post, but let me make a few quick observations:

  - The goal is integration not assimilation. Don't push team members into molds; instead, encourage them to contribute their unique skills and perspectives.

  - Build trust that makes room for frank conversations informed by multiple differing perspectives and opinions.

  - Encourage both autonomous work (like flexible schedules and work from home) and collaboration (*ad hoc* groups and projects).

- **Explain the mechanics of working in the organization.** Help them understand the org chart (bosses, peers, and subordinates), how to access benefits (insurance, retirement, and PTO), how to use the technology (equipment and access to data), and how to navigate the physical facilities.

- **Explain how they can leave their mark on the organization.** We all want to impact our corner of the world. Help new team members block out time for deep work. Ask what "flow" typically looks like for them. Explain big problems and big opportunities that exist in your industry and your company and encourage them to engage in the discussion. Ask new team members to be on the lookout for ways to do things better, faster, and cheaper. Encourage team members to speak to problems and opportunities that are outside their discipline. Explain how to communicate ideas to pivotal people in the organization.

- **Explain how to "pull the ripcord."** Even with rigorous screening, hiring, and onboarding processes, occasionally you'll make a hire that just doesn't work. Explain to the team member what to do if they feel like the new job is just not working out.

Check in periodically in the first few weeks to make sure the new team member is productive, connected, and well informed.

WEEK 18 :: GOVERNANCE :: LEGAL ORGANIZATION

This week's One-Year, Thirty-Minute Business Transformation isn't too sexy, but it could

- impact your ability to shield yourself, your family, and your assets from legal liability;

- impact your ability to raise capital for your business;

- impact your personal tax liability and more.

My purpose this week isn't to offer advice because the topic is outside my area of expertise. The real answers will have to come from your accountant and/or tax attorney. My purpose this week is to offer education and encourage you to consider your options for the legal organization of your company.

Typically, most small business are legally organized one of these five ways:

Sole Proprietorship

Sole proprietorships are the simplest form of business organization. They do not produce a separate business entity but can register a separate trade name (Super Good Plumbing vs. Jim Smith, Plumber). Business assets and liabilities are mingled with personal assets and liabilities. Consequently, sole proprietors can be held financially liable for business debts and can be held personally liable for the actions of the business (which could put personal assets at risk). Sole proprietors can sometimes have greater difficulty in raising money than those who choose other business organizations.

Partnership

This is for a business owned by two or more individuals. In *general partnerships,* partners share profits, losses, and liability. In *limited partnerships,* one partner has control of the operation and bears unlimited liability while the other partner(s) contribute(s), shares profits, and has limited liability. Limited Liability Partnerships (LLP) give limited liability to each partner, protecting them from the actions of other partners. Partnerships can sometimes more effectively raise money (versus sole proprietors) since lenders can consider the combined creditworthiness of all partners.

Limited Liability Companies

Limited Liability Companies (LLC) are hybrids of partnerships and corporations. They allow owners to protect their personal assets by separating them from the business's assets. They also protect owner's assets in the event someone sues the business. Business profits and losses are passed through to the owner's personal income. Members of an LLC are considered self-employed.

Corporation

A corporation is an entity unto itself, separate from its owners. It can own assets, sell assets, sue, be sued, and sell part of itself to other entities (stockholders). The corporation is responsible for its own debts and liabilities. Shareholders are protected from liability, but should the corporation become worthless (loss of all asset value, bankruptcy, a large legal judgment, etc.), the shareholder's stock could be worth nothing. There are several flavors of corporations, but here are three common ones.

- *C Corp* is owned by shareholders and is taxed as its own entity. In some cases, the profits are taxed twice: the corporation pays taxes, and, when dividends are paid to shareholders, they are taxed again when the shareholder pays personal taxes. C Corps can raise money through the sale of stock.

- *S Corp* is owned by shareholders, but profits are passed through to shareholders to be taxed at each shareholder's individual tax rate. There are limits on the number of shareholders in an S Corp.

- *B Corp* are for-profit entities, but shareholders hold the company accountable to make some tangible public benefit besides making a profit. Some states require an annual filing that documents their public benefit.

Cooperative

Cooperatives are owned and operated by those who benefit from its services. Profits are disbursed to the members of the cooperative. A frequent use of cooperatives is farmers banding together to market their products as one entity to regular buyers—distributors, grocery store chains, and food service suppliers.

If you want more detail, check out the Small Business Administration Page on business structure at https://www.sba.gov/business-guide/launch-your-business/choose-business-structure.

This week's exercise is to consider what you've just read and examine, with your accounting and tax advisers, whether or not you can find more favorable tax treatment, better financial resources, better protection for personal assets, better options for employee compensation, or any other additional benefits by changing your legal structure.

WEEK 19 :: FINANCE :: FINANCIAL LITERACY

If you want employees to make decisions like you make decisions, they're going to need access to the same data you have, and they're going to need to know how to make sense of that data. That includes a big dose of Financial Literacy.

Rudimentary financial literacy doesn't require that everyone in the organization take an accounting class, and it doesn't mean that everyone knows what everyone else makes. Basic financial literacy rallies everyone in the organization around common goals, gives them a common language, and increases their value to the organization.

This week's One-Year, Thirty-Minute Business Transformation lays out the first financial literacy concepts that everyone in your organization should understand and gives some ideas on how to begin financial literacy education in the organization.

Profitability is built on creating an *economic value surplus*. The formula is as follows.

$$Revenue \text{ (units sold * price per unit)}$$
$$- Cost\ of\ Goods\ Sold \text{ (materials + labor)}$$
$$- Fixed\ Costs$$
$$= Profit$$

It's important for your team to understand each of these components. *Revenue* is a combination of two things—*volume* and *price*. The price for your good or service must be enough to cover the cost of goods sold (the materials and labor required to make the product). The remaining money, in aggregate, must be enough to cover the *fixed costs* of the business (rent, utilities, insurance, phones, desks, trucks, office supplies, and more). Volume represents the number of people that are interested and willing to pay for your good or service at the price you've established. The money left over after paying the cost of goods sold and the overhead expenses is *profit*. The accumulated profit must be enough to build a surplus, so the business can survive temporary downturns in volume or can capitalize on emerging opportunities.

The real magic happens when team members see how their day-to-day responsibilities drive each of these components. Price must be high enough to cover the fixed and variable costs and must also create a favorable value proposition for the customer (the price paid must be equal to the benefit derived by the customer). Pricing plays into decisions on marketing and advertising.

Cost of goods sold represents an incredible opportunity for inviting team members into financial literacy. If they can streamline the creation of the good or service, it drives the labor cost per unit down, allowing the company to make more units in the same amount of time. That increases profitability. If they can negotiate more favorable rates with suppliers, driving the cost of materials down, that increases profitability. If they can obtain higher quality materials for the same price, thus increasing quality and lowering the defect or warranty rate, that increases profitability. Greater profitability enables the company to create a larger surplus and be more prepared to weather economic storms. The COVID-19 crisis showed us the importance of financial resilience. A report by JP Morgan Chase found that only half of all small businesses had enough cash on hand to survive for twenty-seven days.

Fixed costs are those incurred by the business just by being open: rent, utilities, insurance, and more. When team members understand how coworking or working from home can lessen the need for office space, pushing rents down, or how staying healthy can help push down insurance costs, they begin to get an understanding of the financial calculations that you are making every day. That understanding leads to engagement and empathy.

These actions move team members to the same side of the equation as owners. Instead of owners being adversaries (i.e., the employee's loss is the owner's gain), team members are now rowing in the same direction as the owners because they understand the owner's endgame: building a viable, sustainable, and stable enterprise that can continue to offer employment and opportunity for years to come.

So where do you start? First, I'd convene a meeting with all employees (if the company size allows it. If not, do several meetings) and explain the economic value surplus equation above. Explain that from this time forward, you're going to share some of the company's financial information, so they can see how these pieces work. Then, ask for their help in increasing revenue and decreasing expense. Finally, explain what's in it for them. I'd suggest giving them skin in the game. If revenue increases, expense decreases, and/or profitability increases (whatever information you're willing to share), give them a cut of the savings or profitability. You've now created common goals and explained it with what is now common language. You're on your way.

Reconvene the meeting each month and report results.

Where do you go next? I'd suggest explaining double entry accounting, that every financial transaction is recorded in two ways. When you sell a product, cash is debited, and revenue is credited. When you buy copy paper, cash is credited, and office supplies are debited. This prepares team members for the next, very important step.

Introduce the three primary financial reports: the *Income Statement*, *Balance Sheet*, and *Cash-Flow Statement*.

The Income Statement (sometimes referred to as Profit and Loss Statement or P&L) reports income and expenses for the business for a time period.

The Balance Sheet shows the organization's financial health by tracking what the company owns and owes.

The Cash-Flow Statement shows the movement of money in and out of the business. It differs from the Income Statement because all money coming into a business might not be income. For example, if a company takes out a loan, it receives money but did not generate any income. Conversely, if a company pays back a loan, it spent money but did not incur an expense. Instead, it decreased a liability.

In your thirty-minute exercise this week, decide how you can best engage your team in financial literacy by inviting them into some of the difficult decisions you make on a daily basis.

WEEK 20 :: VALUE CREATION :: ECONOMIC VALUE

Earlier in the One-Year, Thirty-Minute Business Transformation (week eleven) we examined *Experiential Value Creation*, the gap between what the customer pays for our product or service and the utility and enjoyment they experience from the purchase. The goal is to widen that gap as much as possible, so the customer's enjoyment of their purchase far exceeds their monetary investment. In that exercise, we explained the three ways that customers interact with purchases and how to maximize those interactions to create the greatest experiential value. Experiential value creation involves the sometimes subjective evaluation of customers.

This week's One-Year, Thirty-Minute Business Transformation is the purely objective exercise of economic value creation. *Economic Value Creation* is the gap between the sales price of our product or service and the cost to produce that product or service.

In economic value creation, we want to push the *Sales Price* and the *Cost* as far apart as possible until profit is maximized. This is the money we get to keep. There are two important considerations in profit maximization. There is an upper limit to the sales price. Certainly, experiential value is an important part of the equation, but there are mechanical considerations as well. If you raise prices too high, you invite competitors who will enter at a lower price point. Your product or service might be superior, but because your price point is too high, your offering is not even considered. If you cut costs by reducing the quality of your offering (e.g., substandard materials, shoddy workmanship, or reduced reliability), you can do irreparable damage to your reputation.

Costs fall into two categories, *variable* and *fixed*. Variable costs (expressed as cost of goods sold when broken down by sold unit) are those costs that go up and down based on the number of times the product or service is delivered: Every cheeseburger sold, for example, has a bun, a piece of cheese, a hamburger patty, a squirt of mustard, three pickle slices, a wax paper wrapper, and four minutes of employee time devoted to frying, dressing, wrapping, and delivering the finished product. Every therapy session has fifty-five minutes of the counselor's time. The more times the product or service is delivered, the more costs we incur. Fixed costs are those we incur simply by being open. If we serve two or two hundred customers, those costs do not change. Rent, utilities, communications, hardware, software, and insurance typically fall into this bucket.

Variable Costs (Cost of Goods Sold)	**Fixed Costs**
Materials	Building
Labor	Equipment
Transportation	Insurance
	Admin

This week's exercise is devoted primarily to variable costs, but certainly attention should be devoted to reducing fixed costs. We should be regularly checking price vs. value on our office space, insurance, technology, and more.

I want to discuss variable costs in the context of the *Value-Creation Chain.*

Inputs > Transformation Activities > Outputs

Here are a couple of samples of value creation chains from very different industries.

Bakery

Inputs	*Transformation Activities*	*Outputs*
Bakers	Mixing	Cakes
Kitchen Equipment	Stirring	Cookies
Recipes	Baking	Brownies
Flour	Decorating	Pies
Sugar	Packaging	
Eggs		
Baking Soda		
Baking Powder		
Cocoa		
Vanilla		

Hospitals

Inputs	*Transformation Activities*	*Outputs*
Sick people	Consultation	Well people (or at least on the road to health)
Medical professionals (nurses, doctors, lab technicians, therapists, etc.)	Testing	
	Surgery	
Point of service (physical location or virtual meeting)	Therapy	
	Administering medicine	
Medical equipment	General care	
Pharmaceuticals		

Economic value creation improves by moving through the value-creation chain *better, faster, and cheaper.*

One manifestation of "better" can be *quality*, which could be evidenced by fewer defects (i.e., your quality control people find fewer parts that don't meet your specifications or that need to be reworked). "Better" could also mean that the raw materials are free from problems. That opens up the entire vendor or supplier discussion: Do all of the vendor's raw materials for your product perform as expected? Is the quality consistent, or do they vary wildly from batch to batch? Do you have tools in place to measure vendor performance, so you can identify underperforming vendors and defective batches? Do you have initiatives in place that stop or reduce defects in the process? Initiatives that keep your production people from making mistakes? If you've visited someone in the hospital lately and been there when the nurse has administered medication, you've seen a procedure that makes patient care "better": the nurse scanned the wristband on the patient's arm, then scanned a barcode on the medicine they were about to administer. That allows the EMR system to alert them if a wrong medication is about to be given to the patient. "Better" might be more effective use of personnel, materials, or machinery. In short, "better" can represent exploiting a host of operational opportunities.

The second improvement you can make in the value-creation chain is "faster." "Faster" is desirable for several reasons. First, it hastens the moment you get paid. If you can put a product in a customer's hand quicker, you can be paid quicker. I realize that collecting money, paying for raw materials on terms, and credit card processing times all constitute a bunch of moving parts when it comes to money, but suffice it to say, faster is almost always better. Faster on the shop floor means that the same resource can do more work in the same amount of time. If you can automate or organize so that a worker can make ten widgets in an hour instead of eight, you can significantly increase profitability. Any time you can create more units of output with the same units of input with no degradation in quality, that's a good thing. "Faster" also applies in the delivery of raw materials before transformation and delivery after the product is transformed. I know that most of us automatically switch into manufacturing mode when we're talking about transformation activities, but let me remind you of the value of faster when it comes to stroke treatment. If you can begin the transformation activities (i.e., treatment) faster, the patient's prognosis improves dramatically, since during a stroke, 1.9 million neurons die every minute. Speed is almost always a competitive advantage.

The final improvement you want to make in the value-creation chain is "cheaper." This probably seems like a no-brainer, and it is. You certainly want to cut the cost of your processes anytime you can. "Cheaper" can translate into higher margins or in the ability to reduce prices to consumers, making your product or service more competitive and hopefully driving more volume. Certainly, improvements in speed as we discussed earlier can cut costs, but there are other opportunities for cheaper as well—more preferable pricing from vendors, cheaper transportation costs before and after the transformation activities, and lowering administrative costs (that are typically spread across all produced units).

For this week's thirty-minute exercise, map your value-creation chain.

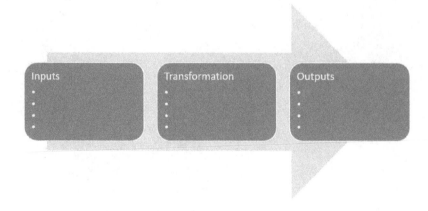

How can inputs be obtained faster or cheaper? How can you keep a minimal number of inputs on hand (saving on inventory holding costs) while still making sure you never impact the ability to start the value-creation process? If the input is a skilled employee, how can you develop and help them become better? How can transformation activities become more streamlined? Be more accurately measured? Require less rework? Be touched by fewer people? How can outputs be delivered to the final customer quicker or in a more convenient way?

Explain the value-creation chain to the people involved in each of these steps. Ask them to critically examine their responsibilities in the light of "better," "faster," and "cheaper." Offer them financial incentives when their recommendations for improvement drive more money to the bottom line.

WEEK 21 :: MARKETING :: SOCIAL MEDIA

Unless your current and potential clients constitute a very obscure part of the business-to-consumer or business-to-business landscape, you need an effective social media presence. Look at these statistics from Hootsuite (a social media management tool vendor):

(Source: https://blog.hootsuite.com/social-media-statistics-for-social-media-managers/.)

- 50 percent of the global population (3.8 billion people) uses social media

- 84 percent of people with access to the internet use social media

- In 2019, people spent, on average, two hours and twenty-four minutes on social media every day

- The average social media user has 8.3 different social accounts

- 43 percent of internet users use social media for work purposes

- 43 percent of internet users use social media to research potential purchases

- 90 percent of internet users say they watch video online at least once a month

- Social ad spending is forecast to increase 20 percent to $43 billion USD in 2020

- Active users by platform

    - Instagram – 1 billion

    - Facebook – 2.5 billion

    - Twitter – 152 million

    - YouTube – 2 billion

    - Pinterest – 335 million

    - LinkedIn – 675 million

    - Snapchat – 218 million

    - TikTok – 800 million

This week's One-Year, Thirty-Minute Business Transformation exercise is to reexamine your social media strategy. Some of you might have ignored this marketing, messaging, and customer service channel, but you're probably ignoring it at your own peril. Your customers, potential customers, and competitors are most likely already there. Some of you might be active in social media but are not maximizing the results. Some of you might be knocking it out of the park.

There are two things that are unique and wonderful about social media. The first thing is that the best social media content is "useful." The plumber is posting a list of the ten worst foods for clogging garbage disposals. The chiropractor is sharing an infographic on how to lift heavy items without hurting your back. You'll occasionally see a "hard sell" on social media, but they aren't prevalent. The second thing is that, unlike almost every other marketing and advertising medium, social media is a conversation: business-to-customer, customer-to-business, and customer-to-customer (in front of the business). And those conversations are enabled and encouraged by the platform provider. Some platforms include tools that help the customer rate, review, and recommend the business.

One more thing before jumping into this week's exercise. Some business own-ers and managers live in fear of what might be posted on social media. They dread the one-star review or the lengthy post from the irate customer. That content represents one of the best opportunities on social media. Customers don't expect companies to be perfect, but they do expect companies to make things right when they make a mistake. When the poor review or the flam-ing complaint comes, jump right in. Apologize for the missed expectation, commit to making it right, and give the complaining customer the first step in repairing the relationship.

I recommend something like this, "Jim Smith, I am sorry that was your experience in our office. We want every customer to feel like they were treated well and received incredible value by purchasing our product. I'd like to talk with you about your experience. Would you call me at 888-555-5555 or email me at johnjones@email.com, so we can see what happened?" Again, in front of this complaining customer, all your other customers, and any potential customers, you've voiced your commitment to making this right. If you're able to resolve the complaining customer's problem, invite them back to the post to share the resolution (without all the gory details).

Let's jump into this week's exercise.

Create a social media manifesto.

- Describe what you want to accomplish (position my company as an expert in the field; showcase the talented people on my team; generate sales leads; provide industry and company information so people can understand what we do; sell products or services online)

- Define what winning looks like (reach, number of views, number of followers, and/or number of engagements—that is, clicks, likes, replies, pins, and/or saves—number of leads, number of mentions, number of tags, and/or number of reposts, shares, or retweets)

- Identify six to eight themes that you want to consistently communicate (these might revolve around core values, products, people, and/or community involvement)

Stake out your place on social media. I suggest creating accounts on the platforms you think you might want to use, just so you have the account name claimed. You can build them out as it makes sense (you have a plan that fits the platform, the ability to create meaningful content, and the bandwidth to interact with customers on the platform).

Identify the best place or places to talk to your customers and potential customers on social media. If you don't know where they hang out on social media, ask them. Each social media network has detailed demographics of its users. Review those and see if your customers are there.

Create a social media calendar. Using the themes from your manifesto, create a content calendar with dates, platforms, and messages. Content can be original (created by you or your team) or curated (useful to your audience and consistent with the messages of the manifesto but created by someone else). Schedule in "big" content and the run up to it. For example, if you're going to be at a trade show, announce it in advance, ask followers to meet you there (scheduling appointments would be great), show pictures of preparation, and broadcast live from the event when you get there. Track results from the content you share. Check levels of engagement and use it to refine future content. Periodically extend the invitation for more interaction outside of social media (if that makes sense in your business model).

Execute. Social media requires consistent care and feeding. Create good content, consistently share it, track the results, and engage with your audience.

This is the most rudimentary of social media information. There's much more to learn if you want to go deeper. Here are some good resources if you want to take your research further.

https://www.socialmediaexaminer.com/
https://www.socialfresh.com/
https://socialmediaexplorer.com/
https://www.marismith.com/
https://sproutsocial.com/

WEEK 22 :: STRATEGIC PLANNING :: MERGERS AND ACQUISITIONS

Mergers and acquisitions are things that multi-billion-dollar companies do, right? Certainly, companies of that size do merge with and acquire other companies, but these strategies can be employed by companies of almost any size.

In this week's One-Year, Thirty-Minute Business Transformation, we want to dig into the mechanics of mergers and acquisitions—surveying the competitive landscape, identifying synergies that might exist between us and our competitors, and crafting a plan to bring two businesses together.

Let's do a quick definition of terms. In a *merger*, two equals come together and craft a new business entity that most likely features leadership from both businesses, products from both businesses, and a consolidated customer base. In an *acquisition*, one business purchases the assets, products, and customer base of another business. It's possible that the leadership of the acquired business will be no longer be present. Its brand might be swallowed completely by the acquiring business.

Before we jump into this week's exercise, let's lay out the case for a merger or acquisition:

- Consolidated back office functions reduce cost. Two HR departments become one, two finance departments become one, etc.

- Distinctive competencies of each entity are leveraged across the new entity.

- The new entity has a broader product offering.

- Market share for the new entity automatically increases.

- It reduces rivalry in the industry.

- It increases bargaining power with vendors and customers.

Here are a few observations before we start on the exercise:

- Companies who have grown rapidly through mergers and acquisitions all say the same thing: nothing is more important than culture fit. If the cultures of the merging companies clash, the synergy never happens and value dissipates, sometimes costing companies incredible amounts of money to separate the entities. Occasionally the companies don't survive.

- Merging companies operationally is hard. There are systems and processes that must be combined. Which accounting system will the new entity use? How will we reconfigure the sales pipeline? And much, much more.

- Most likely, some people will lose their job. That's part of the improved value proposition. You need to create a separation process that, as much as possible, allows departing people to keep their dignity, positions them for future success, and gives them adequate financial resources for a transition. You also need a plan for the people who are staying and are grieving the loss of their coworkers.

- You might be looking at your bank account and thinking, "I can't acquire a box of pencils, let alone another company." You might be surprised. There might be companies you could acquire for just an assumption of debt or for a stream of future payments instead of a lump sum upfront.

- Acquire or merge with positive cash flow. A company with negative cash flow might seem like an easy acquisition target, but unless the reason for negative cash flow is readily apparent and easily fixable, you want to acquire or merge with a company that is "paying its own way."

- If you're acquiring a company just for their book of business, be cautious. Unless the company has a locked-in customer base (e.g., the only factory-authorized service center for XYZ brand widgets in six states), customers could defect to competitors and significantly diminish the value of the acquisition.

- I understand that every bullet point above this seems fraught with peril. These are two hard strategies and they require a lot of soul-searching and empirical analysis before they are utilized. But, when executed correctly, they can create incredible value and opportunity for the owners and companies who utilize them. Companies can quickly experience every one of the benefits spelled out earlier in the post.

Here's this week's thirty-minute exercise:

- List three to five merger or acquisition targets. Remember, you're looking for culture fit, complementary product offerings, and organizational synergy. When thinking about complementary products, consider adjacent industries. For example, an HVAC company might find a good merger/acquisition target with a plumber.

- Write a few notes after each one regarding why you think they make a good merger or acquisition target. Be specific. Cite products, services, people, similar marketing communication, etc.

- Sleep on it for a night or two. Revisit the list and your notes and see if they still make sense.

- If your idea still makes sense in a day or two, share it with a couple of trusted lieutenants in your organization and get their take. Discuss all of the challenges listed above and any additional ones that you identify.

If after this internal deliberation, you still think it's a promising idea, these are your next steps:

- Initiate a conversation with the principal of the target company. Suggest lunch or coffee. This is your first opportunity to gauge the culture of the organization because culture flows down from the top.

- If the conversation is positive, introduce the merger/acquisition topic. If there is interest from both sides, sign a mutual nondisclosure agreement. This will ensure that any financials or trade secrets disclosed during the following discussions will remain private.

- Arrange a meeting with a small group from both entities. Invite operations people, finance people, and tech people. In this meeting, you're still checking for culture fit, and you're starting to dig into overarching operational questions. It might be a good idea to engage a third party to manage this meeting. Their job is to make sure everyone's concerns are aired and addressed.

- Each entity needs to debrief after this meeting to discuss culture, markets, operations, finance, and tech.

- If everyone involved is still feeling positive, it's time to involve legal counsel, accountants, and possibly consultants with experience in merging operations (if you haven't involved them up until now).

This One-Year, Thirty-Minute Business Transformation was a thought-starter for one of the more ground-shifting topics in the series. If you decide to undertake one of these strategies, think long and hard, and get help.

WEEK 23 :: PEOPLE :: EMPLOYEE DEVELOPMENT

Nobody wants to be a screwup at their job. In fact, according to Dan Pink's excellent 2009 book *Drive*, the social sciences teach us that one of the three things people seek in their work is *Mastery*. Pink briefly describes mastery as "the urge to get better and better at something that matters."

There are two things that you, as an employer, can do to tap into an employee's intrinsic desire for mastery—(1) provide resources, time, and support for the employee's self-initiated efforts for personal and professional growth and (2) build an effective employee development program inside the organization.

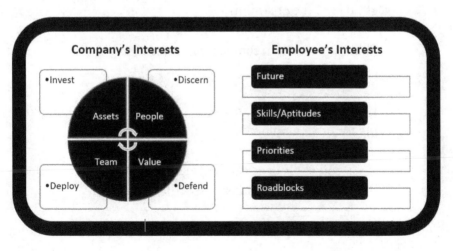

Effective employee development programs align the interests of the employee with the interests of the company. With an effective employee development program, you are, concurrently, making a better person and a better employee.

This week's One-Year, Thirty-Minute Business Transformation exercise is to design a framework to start your program. The graphic above will provide direction.

The company's interest in the employee can be view through four lenses:

- **Employees as assets to be developed**. Answer these questions:

  - What resources can we provide to make this employee more valuable to the organization (such as formal education, additional experiences inside the organization, continuing education units (CEUs), professional certifications, webinars, or industry meetings)?

  - How will this employee's compensation reflect their additional value to the organization?

  - What should the accompanying gains in productivity or value creation look like?

  - How can we leverage this employee's new skills into mentoring for other employees?

  - What soft skills does this employee need to develop in addition to technical or industry-specific skills?

- **Employees as people to be understood.** Answer these questions:

– How does this employee embody the organization's core values?

– How does this employee embrace the organization's culture?

– What motivates this employee in addition to or instead of monetary compensation? Pink's book tells us they want *autonomy* (a measure of control over their work), *mastery* (the opportunity to improve their work skills), and *purpose* (a feeling that their work has meaning beyond a paycheck).

- **Employees as team members to be deployed.** Answer these questions:

– How well is this employee suited to their current position?

– If the employee is not well suited, can they be coached or transferred?

– If they no longer fit in the organization, should they be terminated?

– Is the employee trusted by other team members?

– Does the employee skillfully navigate conflict?

– Does the employee take responsibility for mistakes without making excuses?

– Does the employee respect and learn from the diverse viewpoints of other team members?

– Does the employee display good absorptive capacity for new ideas, procedures, and environments?

- Does the employee have a mentor mindset?

- **Employees as indispensable.** Answer these questions:

  - Are there employees who, if they left, would put the health of the organization in jeopardy?

  - How can you most quickly mitigate this risk with additional hiring, training, or outsourcing?

The employee's interest can be viewed through four lenses:

- **What does my future look like?**

  - Is there a career path here for someone with my interests and skills?

  - If so, what does it look like?

  - What happens if my interests change over time (e.g., I want to move from IT to sales)?

  - Is there a path for advancement for a skilled practitioner that doesn't include management?

  - What is the company's policy on intellectual property?

- **Can I learn and grow in the organization (skills, aptitudes, and experiences)?**

  - Will you invest in my growth?

  - If so, how?

- Will I be mentored?

- Will you give me opportunities to try my hand at several things?

- Will I have the opportunity to work in other parts of the country or other countries?

- **Can I keep my priorities intact if I work here?**

  - Can I live the way I want to live (core values, hours, time off, great coworkers, benefits that are important to me, etc.)?

  - Will the organization morph as my life changes, realizing that my priorities might have to change over the course of my employment (children, illness, aging parents, etc.)?

- **Will the organization help me navigate roadblocks as they surface?**

  - Can I escape a boss that isn't committed to my development?

  - Can I recover from involvement in a failed project?

Use the section above to construct two things: a questionnaire for employees and an initial outline of the growth opportunities you can include in your employee development program. Once your employee questionnaire is done, begin meeting with employees one by one and gather their responses. Take their feedback and revisit your initial employee development plan. Add items that are important to employees (and fit in your budget) but were absent from your original list. Remove items that, based on your interviews, are not important to employees.

Begin rolling out your plan. The conversations should be something like, "You said you were interested in balanced scorecards. If we had a balanced scorecard in our organization, that would be great. If I sent you to a class for balanced scorecards, would you come back and work with me personally to make one for the company? When we're done, I'd like for you to present to all the department heads and explain our work. Would you be up for that?"

Have a conversation like this with everyone on your team. When you knock out one of the things important to the employee and the company, move to the next thing and keep the growth going.

WEEK 24 :: BUSINESS CONTINUITY :: OPERATIONS

2020 was the poster child for disruption. Between a global pandemic, localized protests and vandalism, and a contentious election in the US where partisan conversations crept into the workplace, business owners and managers faced situations they most likely had never faced before. These events and the fallout from them have magnified the importance of a solid business continuity plan.

In the second One-Year, Thirty-Minute Business Transformation, we discussed business continuity in the context of protecting the data that powers your organization. This week we turn our attention to operations.

Let's jump into the exercise.

People
Operations pivot on people and on the skills they bring to the workplace. To mitigate people risk in the context of business continuity, start here:

- Identify any processes that are not thoroughly documented. If a current employee becomes unavailable, it's imperative that the processes surrounding their job are accurately and thoroughly recorded. Document not just what they do but why it is done, when it is done (including deadlines), and to whom the finished work product is distributed. During this week's thirty-minute exercise, you won't be able to complete the documentation itself, but you want a complete list of all undocumented or underdocumented processes in the organization.

- Identify options for completing critical work if a large percentage of your workforce is unavailable (as we saw with COVID-19).

  - Can work be completed by other personnel?

  - Are those personnel cross-trained, and do they have access to the process documentation from the previous step?

  - Can you access contractors, temp workers, or consultants to complete critical work?

  - If so, who are those people and how quickly can you mobilize them?

- If your workforce is formally organized (unionized), work pro-actively before a work stoppage to engineer an agreement that allows the company and the unionized workers to benefit from the company's success.

- Make training an ongoing part of the company's employee development process so that all workers are continually honing their skills and building a broader base of expertise.

Infrastructure

Clearly, some businesses, like hotels, are location dependent, and remote work is not an option. But for many other businesses, work can be portable. Depending on the nature of the event that triggers use of the business continuity plan, there are multiple options.

- If on-site work is required, and the primary location is destroyed or inaccessible, a *hot site* can be activated. Typically, hot sites are abbreviated replicas of a primary location complete with equipment and tech. In the event of a disaster, the hot site is activated, and workers report to the new site and begin work. Cloud-based systems are accessed from the hot site location, and business continues as usual. Obviously, an expensive solution but sometimes necessary.

- If your business is multilocation, consider moving operations to what would normally be a branch office.

- If the need will be longer term (maybe due to something like a fire or flood), consider a coworking space for temporarily housing your operations.

- In a world of ubiquitous broadband internet service, cloud-based systems, and video conferencing, working from home is a more than viable option. If you don't have a work-from-home policy, work-from-home procedures, or tech that supports work-from-home activity, add the development of those things to your to-do list during this week's exercise. Once you have those things in place, schedule some practice work-from-home days to make sure everything functions as it should.

Resources

There are multiple critical path resources in a business. The absence of any of them can diminish or destroy the organization's value-creation activity. Effective business continuity planning puts those resources back in play as soon as possible, ideally without any interruption to value-creation activities.

- If your organization is dependent on specialty vehicles or other large equipment for which rentals are not available (e.g. tow trucks), craft a plan with a competitor for a shared business continuity plan. You'll be each other's back up, and you'll do a prenegotiated revenue share.

- If your organization uses specialty tools, and those tools become damaged or destroyed, identify multiple sources for replacement tools.

- Identify multiple vendors for raw materials. Craft agreements with primary, secondary, and even tertiary vendors for essential items. Nurture the relationships so that each one represents a win-win for both parties. If a primary vendor fails, make it easy for the other vendors to respond quickly. Always track vendor performance in pricing, quality, and service.

Finance
Even a brief business disruption can have an oversized impact on sales revenue. Unchecked discretionary spending can quickly deplete cash reserves. Activating the business continuity plan might have its own built-in costs (rental charges, overtime, etc.), so acting quickly is a necessity.

- Build a cash reserve much like you'd do for your household. Having three to six months of fixed costs plus all "automatic" business-continuity expenses is a good start.

- Quickly assess the severity (and anticipated length) of the disruption. If necessary, quickly stop all discretionary spending.

Communication
Create a communication procedure as part of the business continuity plan. Where do team members go to get the most up-to-date and best information. Who do they contact if they have questions?

One Final Tool
For the final part of this week's exercise, I'd encourage you to conduct a "premortem." We know all about postmortems from every episode of *CSI* (or one of its spinoffs) that we've watched. When someone dies, the coroner examines them closely to determine the cause of death. A premortem

is similar except, for purposes of this exercise, we propel ourselves into the future and pretend that our business continuity plan has failed miserably. Then, we ask, "What did we miss?" "What fell through the cracks?" "What procedure broke down?" "Who was unprepared and why?" "How did we fail the customer?" You get the idea. It's looking backward at the event from an imagined failed future state. Anything that helps us create another perspective of our response to the disruption is beneficial. Take the results of the premortem and work them back into your business continuity plan.

After you have the plan in place, review it with your team and put a reminder on your calendar to review it every six months to make sure everything still makes sense.

WEEK 25 :: OPERATIONS :: PROCESSES

If you want to be tied to your desk, be forced to solve every problem yourself, never enjoy a day off, and worry constantly about whether or not work is done the way you want it done, ignore this week's One-Year, Thirty-Minute Business Transformation.

Creating processes is the key to delivering a great customer experience, ensuring quality, scaling your business, decreasing mistakes and defects, empowering employees, and increasing velocity.

New business owners struggle with early hires. To the detriment of the organization, they often hire people "just like them," so they can feel confident that the work will be done just like they would do it. The better alternative is to create detailed processes for everything so that every new hire, as they follow the processes, can do the work just as the founder intended. Then, as new talent is added to the organization, those with different skill sets, personalities, and gifts can add new strength to the organization and bring increased clarity and refinement to the processes.

Let's quickly clarify the distinction between *processes* and *policies*. Processes are for those tasks where there is no wiggle room—the way we mass-produce widgets, the way we pay a vendor invoice, or the way we complete new employee documentation. Policies are for those tasks where there might be some gray areas—when do we give a refund, when do we allow a reservation to be cancelled without a cancellation fee, or how many bereavement days do we allow when an employee's family member dies. Processes are like railroad tracks: you can't veer at all from the track without negative consequences. Policies are like guardrails: if you drive anywhere between them, you're safe. With processes, follow the letter of the law. With policies, follow the spirit of the law.

Back to this week's exercise. In thirty minutes, you won't be able document all the vital processes in your organization. So instead, we want to construct the framework that you're going to use to create your process documentation. For processes to be most effective, they must be complete and have sufficient granularity for those who have to follow them.

Here are some suggestions for putting your process documentation together:

- Why does this process exist? What is the endgame? Is it part of a larger task (for example, if this is the process for invoicing a customer, how and where does it fit in the larger task of obtaining, processing, and filling a customer order)?

- Who is responsible for this task? Who is the backup person if the primary person is unavailable?

- What is the requisite knowledge for this task? What is the requisite experience for this task? Where can that knowledge and experience be obtained?

- If the person responsible for this task has a problem or question, who do they ask?

- What resources are required for the task? If software is required for the task, who adds new users or assigns privileges? If there's a software problem, how do you get technical support? If equipment is required, where is it located? Who provides support if the equipment breaks down? If materials are required, where are those materials stored? What vendors supply those materials? What is the process for reordering those materials?

- What are the steps in the process itself? Describe the steps in detail, including why that step is done. As you're documenting the steps, be especially sensitive to the things that are done by instinct or that "everyone knows." Make sure that even the most intuitive, well-known, and obvious things are included in the documentation. For example, if the last step is to drop something in the mail slot, spell out the location of the mail slot.

- Who is notified when the process is completed? How are they notified (even if they are notified automatically via software)? What do those people do with the notification after they have received it?

- How is completion of the process measured? Are the number of widgets manufactured counted? Is the insurance claim reviewed for accuracy? If so, who is responsible for the tracking or auditing the process? How do they give feedback or scoring to the person or people who did the work?

- How is the person executing the process invited into the improvement of the process? How can they question the process or recommend changes?

- Where is the most updated copy of the process stored (on paper; a shared drive; collaboration software like Slack, Microsoft Teams, or Basecamp; or another location)? How are any "remote" copies of the process updated when changes to the process are made? How are changes to the process rolled out? What is the training mechanism? (a demonstration, checklist, class, video, podcast, collaboration software, etc.)

Use these suggestions, then add and customize to create your own framework for documenting processes. Then, beginning with the most critical value-creation activities, work your way through all the processes in your organization.

When you're finished, the goal is to create a "company in a box." That is, if someone with the requisite knowledge and experience picked up your process documentation, they would be able to carry out all the core value-creation activities in the company and perform the work just the way the founder intended (with the modifications and enhancements made by other smart staff members along the way).

WEEK 26 :: CULTURE :: IMPERATIVES

"Culture eats strategy for breakfast." This quote from Peter Drucker has surfaced multiple times over the course of the One-Year, Thirty-Minute Business Transformation. The best strategies and tactics are dead on arrival when they're unleashed into a company with a toxic culture. This week, we're focusing on culture for the third time in the series.

During the course of a consulting engagement, I'm occasionally asked if I have a list of cultural imperatives, that is, attitudes, approaches to work, and actions that should absolutely be baked into the DNA of the organization. I do, and we've already talked about two of them in earlier One-Year, Thirty-Minute Business Transformations—Mentor Mindset in week 4 and Lifelong Learning in week 16.

Here's my complete list:

- *Vulnerability.* The shortcut to building trust inside the organization is the willingness to be transparent, admit weakness, and ask for help when we need it. Trust is the currency we spend with one another as we build an effective team.

- *Confront the Brutal Facts.* Jim Collins reminds us that accurately assessing ourselves, our team, our products and services, our operations, our financial situation, and our competitive environment is mandatory. No rose-colored glasses allowed.

- *Sacrifice of Sacred Cows.* No idea, no product, no service, and no "that's the way we've always done it" is out of bounds. Cling tight to core values. Nothing else escapes scrutiny.

- *Team First.* When making decisions, the good of the organization comes first. Self-serving, self-promoting, and personal advantage have no place in the organization. That must apply from the business owner down to the most recent entry-level hire.

- *Learning Orientation.* The minute we think we know it all is the minute the countdown clock to the death of the organization begins. The organization will never grow beyond those who lead it, so we must continue to improve and learn, personally and professionally.

- *Mentor Mindset.* Every team member is there for the good of the other team members. Owners and managers are committed to staff development, teaching not just the "what" but also the "why."

- *Bias for Action.* "Doing" is better than thinking or talking. Dive for the ball when a teammate drops it. If you promise to do something, do it.

- *Overcommunication.* Information is lubrication for the wheels of the organization. Tell what you know, quickly and completely. If owners want employees to make the same decisions they would make, employees need access to the same information the owners have.

Later in the One-Year, Thirty-Minute Business Transformation, at least one of these will merit their own thirty-minute exercise, but that's not the goal of this week's exercise.

Let's jump in.

This week, I want you create your own list of cultural imperatives, those attitudes, approaches to work, actions, and commitments to one another that must be present in your organization. Every organization is different, so your cultural imperatives will be different, but if they truly are imperative—that is, you must have them baked into your corporate DNA or the organization will fail in living out its mission, reaching its vision, and living up to its core values—you must identify them, live them out, talk about them, train on them, and drive them deeper into the fabric of the organization.

One note before you begin. Let's quickly talk about how *core values* differ from *culture*. Core values are the shared, intrinsic beliefs of those in the organization. It might be a love for small-business owners, a passion for camping, a desire to make learning available to those who previously did not have it, or a commitment to treat client resources (such as money, people, and equipment) as if they were your own. Someone who didn't share those beliefs would continually find themselves uncomfortable in the organization. Everyone else would be rowing in harmony with the values, and the outlier would feel like they were being dragged along.

Culture is how we live inside the organization. After we've been admitted by virtue of our shared values, culture is the mashup of our attitudes, approach to work, commitment to one another, commitment to customers, and commitment to the ideals and health of the organization.

So pull out your pen and notepad or open Evernote and begin. I'm giving you six questions as thought starters for identifying your cultural imperatives. Underneath each question, I've included some statements. Some are positive, some are negative, and others are neutral. I'm not asking if they apply in your organization. I'm tossing out examples of attitudes and actions that might be indicative of company culture. I'm wanting you to identify the cultural must-haves you want and possibly identify some current attitudes and behaviors you should jettison.

- What are the nonoptional behaviors in your organization?

  - Show up on time

  - Work hours are flexible as long as the work is done

  - Arrive at meetings on time

  - Always use all your vacation days

  - Never use all your vacation days

  - Work through lunch

  - It's OK to disagree with a superior in a meeting

  - It's never OK to disagree with a superior in a meeting

  - Answer an email no matter what time it comes

  - Only answer emails Monday through Friday

- What are the attitudes you display in your interactions with one another?

  - There's clearly a pecking order, and the highest-paid person's opinion matters most

  - We have a true meritocracy when it comes to opinions, so the best idea wins the argument

  - It's OK to ask for help when I'm stuck

  - Departmental infighting is the order of the day

- We work hard to work as a team. There's no blaming, just solid cross-discipline problem-solving

- We're good with ambiguity. We know there's plenty we don't know and welcome new situations that challenge the status quo

- We're committed to one another. My boss and coworkers have my back

- What is your approach to work?

  - Good enough is good enough. If it's not broke, don't fix it

  - We strive for excellence in everything, and nothing less is acceptable

  - We dive for the ball when someone drops it

  - If someone screws up, it's on them. They bear the consequences of their own mistake

  - Good ideas can come from anywhere

  - All the good ideas come from our creative people. That's their job

  - When we tackle a problem, we do our research. We want to know the truth even if it hurts; that's the only way we can create great solutions

- What is your approach to customers?

  - We take care of each customer like they're the only one

- Some customers are unreasonable, and if they leave, it's OK

- We're always looking for new ways to serve existing customers and gain new customers, making our products and services better

- We want not only our products and services to be superior, but we also want the customer to have a great customer experience

- How do you view the organization?

  - I'm just a small cog in the machinery, doing what I'm told

  - I have a chance to leave my mark in the organization; my work matters

  - There's more going on here than just making money; we're making life better for our customers

  - All the company cares about is money

  - The people who lead the organization fairly balance the interests of employees, customers, and shareholders

- How do you communicate in the organization?

  - There are lots of islands of information

  - There are single points of failure in the organization, people who alone know specific information or how to do that job

  - Information flows freely from the top of the organization down

- Information flows freely from the bottom of the organization up

- Some conversations are off-limits

After you've worked through the questions and have your own personalized list of cultural imperatives, sleep on it for a day or two and review the list. What did you miss?

Then roll out your list to the leaders in your organization. Does it describe the kind of place where they'd be proud to work? If so, why? If not, what needs to be tweaked and why?

The implementation merits its own One-Year, Thirty-Minute Business Transformation, and that will come later, but knowing the kind of workplace you're after is the right place to start.

Here's a sneak peek on implementation. Once you have your culture described, how do you codify it? How do you live it out? How can the leaders in the organization model it? How can you recognize and reward it? How can you extinguish attitudes and behaviors that don't fit? How can you reinforce it in one-on-one and group training? How can you reinforce it in day-to-day work interactions?

WEEK 27 :: FINANCE :: LIFETIME CUSTOMER VALUE

I remember it vividly. I was a freshly minted consultant. It was one of my first engagements. The client's business was growing quickly, but at the end of every month, he barely had any money left.

So I did an individual profit and loss statement for every single customer. I did some quick math, calculated the percent of each revenue dollar (at his current volume) that went to cover fixed costs, and applied the remainder of that dollar to the variable costs associated with each individual customer. Not a perfect methodology, but it worked well for quickly flushing out the problem. Eureka—the lightbulb moment. For every revenue dollar from the client's biggest customer, he was breaking even (the reasons why are interesting, but that's another story for another day). The more this giant customer spent, the more my client "broke even." We applied the same methodology to every other customer and even found a couple of situations where he lost money for every dollar the customer spent.

I'm a strong proponent for a P&L for every customer. I realize it only makes sense in certain industries, but if it works in yours, you should do it.

That's not the topic for this week's One-Year, Thirty-Minute Business Transformation, but that type of math is at the heart of this week's exercise.

In many industries, a company is upside-down financially when they first begin a relationship with a customer. The costs associated with marketing, advertising, selling, onboarding, and servicing the customer the first time exceed the revenue from the customer's initial purchase. Hopefully, just a few purchases in, the company is right-side up and making money. In the course of calculating the acquisition and onboarding costs, the company should be projecting and making customer experience decisions based on the potential Lifetime Value of the Customer. Loyal, happy customers, depending on the industry, could represent a lifetime revenue stream of thousands, tens of thousands, or even hundreds of thousands of dollars. Happy customers tell their friends. That can translate into even more lucrative customers.

This week's One-Year, Thirty-Minute Business Transformation is to identify the factors that constitute the lifetime customer value calculation for your products and services.

Let's jump into this week's exercise.

- *What are the costs associated with acquiring a new customer?* Depending on your industry, it could include items like annual marketing and advertising expenses (divided by the number of new customers each year), direct selling costs (lead generation, sales technology, sales salaries, sales commission, etc.), and on-boarding costs (customer training and installation services).

- *What does the customer pay for the product?*

- *How many times will the customer buy the product?* What is the range from the most sporadic customer to the most loyal customer?

- *What does it cost to produce each copy of the product?* Depending on your product or service, it will include cost of goods sold, plus additional costs for packaging and delivery.

- *What does it cost to service already acquired customers?* There might be customer service calls, technical support calls or costs for billing and collecting.

The math should look something like this:

> Number of times purchased * purchase price
> - number of times purchased * cost of goods sold (and additional costs)
> - initial acquisition costs
> - ongoing support costs
> = *total lifetime value*

You'll probably want to do some math that's similar to what I did in my initial illustration to reduce the top line purchase price number to reflect the impact of fixed costs.

So what do you do with this information once you have it? Here are some questions to help generate ideas:

- What are the primary drivers of purchase frequency? How can we move less frequent purchasers to more frequent purchasers, allowing us to spread the acquisition cost over more units and consequently increase lifetime customer value?

- Can we draw any correlation between purchase frequency and acquisition costs or support costs? Does a more expensive acquisition equal a more frequent purchaser? If so, maybe the extra acquisition cost is desirable. Maybe there's an inverse relationship between frequency and support cost, that is, the more they use the product or service, the less they need support.

- If a customer is ready to defect, what can we do to save them? Is there any correlation between defecting customers and their use of support? Based on their potential lifetime customer value, what can we afford to spend to keep them?

- How can we leverage the personal networks of high total lifetime value customers to find more like them? They should be our best brand ambassadors.

- Since high total lifetime value customers have demonstrated a willingness to spend money with our company, are there other products or services that might be of interest to them?

Once you've completed your exercise, begin educating your team on the importance of lifetime customer value. The first time that new customer walks through the door could be the beginning of a long and profitable relationship. Treat the opportunity that way.

WEEK 28 :: CULTURE :: CHANGE

The Greek philosopher Heraclitus said, "Change is the only constant in life." True when he lived twenty-five hundred years ago. Still true now. That being the case, we ought to be pretty good at it. But we're not. Inevitably, when we introduce change into our organization, it's a struggle.

We like what we know. It's comfortable, and we know what to expect. So when change comes, for a good percentage of us, we dig in our heels. There are a small number of change addicts out there who embrace it, but they are few and far between.

Joseph Schumpeter (1883–1950), an Austrian economist who immigrated to the US and eventually became a US citizen, made a compelling case for change in the workplace. In fact, the change he advocated for was so far reaching, it required periodic "destruction." Schumpeter introduced the idea of *Creative Destruction* in 1942. He taught that if we are making money, competitors will work to find alternative ways to meet those same customer needs, so they can make that money instead of us. So to succeed for the long-term, we must be ever vigilant to look for ways to improve on our work and do a better job of meeting customer needs, sometimes requiring that we blow up what we've done and rebuild it. For a business, it's the ultimate change—shoot the horse you've been riding and get a new horse. Think about the evolution of home entertainment over the last thirty years: VCR to DVD to Blu-ray to streaming services. Each change in technology required companies to abandon formerly revenue-generating products and build new, different ones. Before we move on to this week's One-Year, Thirty-Minute Business Transformation, let's make a quick list of companies who were confronted with a mandate for creative destruction, refused, and subsequently died or are dying now: Kodak, Blockbuster, AOL, Blackberry, Myspace, Xerox, Polaroid, and almost every newspaper in the US.

The goal of this week's exercise is to create a plan you can utilize when you're introducing change into your organization. That change might be as sweeping as replacing a product line that has generated the bulk of your revenue for the past ten years, as far reaching as replacing an enterprise-wide software system, or as personal as changing the health insurance provider in your benefit package. Use the thought starters below (listed in no particular order) and supplement them with your own ideas to create a change management plan that will equip your team for the one constant—change.

- **Start with why.** Change in an organization is never random. Explain the rationale for the change—previously unseen market conditions, changing customer tastes, underperforming vendors, software no longer supported, need new functionality, price, etc.

- **Explain that "here" is unacceptable.** One of the most difficult things I've run across when introducing change into an organization (a regular occurrence in my work) is a longing for the status quo. The status quo sometimes is laden with emotion because it represents the world as designed by a beloved founder (many times a family member). When we introduce change, it seems like we're dismantling the founder's legacy. In reality, change often mirrors the work of the founder: they created the original product or service to meet the needs of the market, and we are honoring their work by recalibrating for the needs of a new market. "Here" is never an acceptable alternative for a business. We must evolve.

- **Change is consistent with mastery.** Everyone wants to be good at their job. As we become better at our craft, we change. We find new ways to do existing work. Introducing change gives us the opportunity to up our game and add new tools to our toolbox.

- **Change is consistent with lifelong learning.** We encourage individual and team growth. Some change is evolutionary; some is revolutionary. When we introduce change into the organization, we add to our collective knowledge base, which allows us to become more effective and efficient and to serve customers more skillfully.

- **Invite people into the process.** As much as possible, involve your team in every part of the change. For example, if you're buying new enterprise software, don't make it solely an IT decision. Invite users from every involved department into the evaluation, buying, implementation, and training process. It will take longer, but employee buy-in will skyrocket.

- **Be vulnerable.** The more complex the change, the more unknowns exist. You and other leaders in the organization don't know everything. It's OK to say, "I don't know" or "I need help."

- **Be transparent.** As change unfolds, be upfront about everything. When a vendor drops the ball, say so. If you decide to delay a portion of the project, don't obfuscate and or make excuses. Trust will grease the wheels of change, and trust comes from transparency and vulnerability.

- **Paint the picture of the future state.** As a leader in the organization, it's imperative that, as part of the "why" you spell out the desired future state that will result from the change. How will the change make the organization healthier? How will the customer experience improve? How will the organization have better data for decision-making? How will employees be better trained or better equipped?

- **Be resolute.** As I wrote this, I almost typed, "Be confident." But in the context of changing the organization, being resolute is better than being confident. The commitment and subsequent actions to see the transformation through to the end is better than rah-rah speeches.

- **Seek and obtain sponsorship.** Don't lead alone during change. Recruit other leaders to join you in bringing change to the organization. Share the vision and project with those who can lead the charge with you. Focus on those who have the biggest stake in the transformation. They will bring along their teams and will influence those on adjacent teams.

- **Make a roadmap.** Identify the beginning, milestones along the way, and the end. Flesh out this schedule with activities, status meetings, status reports, and the people accountable.

- **Communicate.** If this list were in order, this would be close to the top. Communicate before, during, and after every phase in the change process. Communicate information, progress (including milestones reached and missed), and the transformation already happening during the implementation of the change. I like the idea of appointing a scribe for the change process who is separate from the change manager (project manager, CEO, consultant) and the other project sponsors.

- **Celebrate.** When you reach the end and begin to experience transformation in the organization, throw a party. Celebrate those who did the work, the work itself, and the impact you'll have on the organization for years to come.

If you'll use this week's exercise to put together a change management toolbox using these ideas (plus any additional ones you come up with), you'll be ready to lead your organization through the inevitable, necessary changes that will make your organization ready for the future.

WEEK 29 :: GOVERNANCE :: DECISION-MAKING

Over the course of a day, we make hundreds of decisions. Many, in the great scheme of things, are inconsequential—blue shirt or yellow shirt, mustard or mayo, checkout aisle six or eleven. However, when we're at work, some of our decisions might have a bit more impact—this new region, that new region, or both; this new employee or that new employee; abandon this product or invest a bunch of money into marketing it for another quarter or two. These types of decisions affect the lives of people, the trajectory of our company, and the amount of money we make or lose in upcoming quarters.

What if we could get better at Decision-Making? Let's agree up front that every decision carries risk. We can't "good decision" our way out of every fork in the road and remove risk. Most of us fall victim to what those who study decision-making call "resulting." We believe if we get good results, we made a good decision. If we get bad results, we made a bad decision. Let me illustrate. The odds of winning on any given number at the roulette table are one in thirty-seven. If you walk up to the table, place your chips on five, and the little ball goes into the five on the wheel, you might believe you made a good decision. In reality, you made a bad decision (the math was against you) but got a good result. Conversely, if you hire a salesperson with experience in your industry, stellar credentials, and a history of strong sales, and you equip them with every resource they need to sell your product, and they fail miserably, you more than likely made a good decision but got a bad result. Just one of the foibles that we humans struggle with as we evaluate our decisions.

So how do we up our decision-making game? In this week's One-Year, Thirty-Minute Business Transformation, I encourage you to spend your thirty-minute exercise piecing together a decision-making framework that you'll use when your organization is faced with a decision. I'll give you some thought starters and you can grab what works for you and add your own.

- **What empirical data can we bring to bear on the decision?** It's easy to fall in love with people, products, places, and processes. Can we put our hands on data that will give us objective information, such as sales numbers, number of defects, number of returns, sales by location, sales by hour, sales by salesperson, production per assembly line, or bounce rate for the landing page?

- **How can I remove my ego from the decision?** It's tough to divorce yourself from a person or project that you've poured yourself into. In reality, you are not what you do. You still have worth, and you're still smart, even if the object of your affection is looking questionable. Recognize this for yourself and recognize that others in the organization will have similar feelings toward the people and things they've invested in. Step away and help them step away. Two more things on ego. First, we love our own ideas and struggle to see how they might have a couple of holes. Second, we love information (both empirical and anecdotal) that supports our position and tend to discount information that opposes our position. Be on guard against both of these things.

- **Enlist the collective genius of the people most affected by the decision.** If I could list the most frequent management screwups, this would be close to the top—people unfamiliar with the intimate details of the work trying to improve the work. In reality, the people who do the work are most qualified to improve it. Get input from employees, customers, and vendors, whoever can help you assemble the largest body of knowledge on the subject about which you are making a decision. One important thing: an outside perspective does help because people are occasionally so blinded by the forest, they can't see the trees. But I'd err on the side of getting lots of input from those in the know.

- **Get help from someone who's made similar decisions.** The Israelite king Solomon said, "There's nothing new under the sun." True when he wrote it three thousand years ago. Still true now. Find someone who's faced a similar situation and pick their brain.

- **Propel yourself forward and look back.** As much as you can, transport yourself to the end of every fork in the road (all the possible decision options) and look backward. Things might seem much clearer from that perspective—after all, hindsight is 20/20. What would have to go right to get here? What could go wrong on the way to here? Can I live with the consequences of the things that might go wrong? What are the probabilities for each of these things going right or wrong? Conduct a premortem in your head: jump to the end of the decision, assume it failed miserably, then ask, "What did we screw up that caused this?"

- **Would you put money on this?** I wish I could claim credit for this idea, but it comes from Annie Duke's brilliant book, *Thinking in Bets*. She encourages her readers to ask themselves, "Would I bet on this?" This moves the discussion from theoretical to financial. Before we bet on something, we contemplate the probability (e.g., run or pass, cover the spread or not cover the spread). Our emotions (we love our team and hate the other team) are eclipsed by the reality of what could happen to our wallet.

- **Find a contrarian.** Seek out someone to poke holes in the decision you're narrowing in on. They can be inside or outside the organization. Encourage them to pick it apart personnel-wise, strategically, operationally, and financially.

- ***Festina lente.*** Caesar Augustus adopted this motto—"Make haste, slowly." Make decisions quickly but deliberately. Don't fall victim to paralysis by analysis, but don't fire from the hip. Good decision-making is thoughtful and complete but with a bias for action.

Following these steps, or any others for that matter, won't result in perfect decision-making. There's no such thing. We'll still be duped by the poor decisions that have good results (which we'll then believe were good decisions), puzzled by the good decisions that have bad results, and feel smug about the good decisions that yield good results. Our best hope is to optimize our methodology.

WEEK 30 :: MARKETING :: MESSAGING

If there's one business discipline that gives me indigestion, it's marketing. When I sit down to write about strategy or operations, the words flow freely, but when I have to write about marketing or, even worse, prepare marketing materials for my own business, I feel like my IQ drops thirty points.

I know the discipline is vital, so I've enlisted the help of people I trust. You'll find my Kindle full of books from Donald Miller, Seth Godin, Bernadette Jiwa, Jay Baer, and Jonah Berger. People who can help me decide what to say and how to say it. You'll find my recommended reading list at the bottom of this post.

This week's One-Year, Thirty-Minute Business Transformation is devoted to the most rudimentary of marketing disciplines: Messaging, or *What do I say when I talk to potential customers?* I'm afraid we devote too much attention to branding (like logo design and colors) instead of the real words we say to the people we desperately want to talk to.

So my goal for you in this week's thirty-minute exercise is to use the criteria below to evaluate your communication with current and potential customers. Check your website, email campaigns, social media posts, and written materials. These are the some of the most crucial truths I've gleaned from the smart people listed above.

Be brief. People are busy. They scan instead of reading. You've probably got five to ten seconds on your website, one to two seconds for an email subject line, and three to five seconds on a social media post to convince someone to go deeper. On your website, succinctly state the problem you solve, how you solve it, and how the customer's life will be better after consuming your solution. On email and social media, quickly say what the email or post is about and why they should continue reading.

Be clear. Don't be cute; be crystal clear. A clever play on words might be tempting, but a solid message is always better. Don't make the reader work hard to figure out what you're trying to say.

Be valuable. Give value in every interaction. Let current and potential customers know what kind of information and work they can experience when they interact with you or your organization. Give them a taste of the value that will be returned for their investment of time and money.

Solve a problem. Current and potential customers don't really care about you; they care about themselves. How will you resolve an existing issue or make their lives easier, better, or happier?

Be Mick not Rocky. If you're listing the top feel-good movies of all time, and *Rocky* doesn't make the list, you're doing it wrong. The film about a struggling boxer, Rocky Balboa, who finally gets a shot at the title is Hollywood gold. But the pivotal character in the movie isn't Rocky: it's Mick, Rocky's coach, mentor, friend, butt-kicker, and confidant. In your marketing, be Mick the trainer, so your clients can be Rocky the hero.

Be empathetic. Let current and potential customers know that you "get it." You understand their struggles, their frustrations, their obstacles, and their aspirations.

Be trusted. After you've shown that you understand their problems, demonstrate that you know how to solve them. Your proof might be in the form of years of experience, testimonials, or case studies.

Be patient. Don't be the weird person who discusses how many children they want on the first date. Take your time, build trust, ask more questions, and learn everything you can about current and potential customers. Earn the right to heard.

Be transactional. In contrast to the previous question, don't get stuck in the "friend zone." Let potential customers know that the goal of your interactions is a paid engagement. Give potential customers a chance to begin the engagement with early and frequent calls to action. Be ready when they're ready.

Be aspirational. Paint a picture of what their life will look like after using your product or service. Will they have more free time, more money, more security, more piece of mind, happier employees, or better data enabling them to make better decisions?

If you'll critique your communication using just the truths above, you'll remove some clutter and make your message easier to read and easier to act on.

If this whets your appetite to go deeper on your marketing, you'll benefit from these books.

Donald Miller, *Building a Story Brand*
Donald Miller, *Marketing Made Simple*
Seth Godin, *This is Marketing*
Bernadette Jiwa, *Marketing: A Love Story*
Jonah Berger, *Contagious*
Jay Baer, *Youtility*

WEEK 31 :: GOVERNANCE :: PROJECT MANAGEMENT

Every organization, from the solo practitioner to the multi-billion-dollar, publicly traded company has projects. It might be installing new enterprise software, building a branch office, or introducing a new manufacturing process. And, if you have projects, you need a solid project framework.

In this week's One-Year, Thirty-Minute Business Transformation, I'm going to give you factors for successful Project Management, then introduce a simple project management framework. If you don't have an existing project management tool, I encourage you to use your thirty-minute exercise to customize this framework for your organization, then try it out on your next project.

Successful project management is about the stewardship of four resources—*time, materials, money,* and *people.* Materials can take the form of a new software package or a pile of lumber but most always represents an input that must be transformed during the project. People can take the form of employees, contractors, or vendors who must be aligned, informed, and coordinated during the project. But the most important resource is time because you can't make any more of it. There's always a chance to earn more money, procure more materials, and engage more people, but you can't manufacture any more time. Consequently, time is the primary driver in project management.

The crux of good project management is coordinating transformation activities (typically people + materials + time), so they happen on schedule, with sufficient quality, on budget, and in the right order. A critical piece of project management is understanding *predecessor* and *successor* activities. Predecessor activities are those that must either be started or, in some cases, completed before the next activity begins. Successor activities are those that are dependent on a predecessor activity.

There are a host of software tools that can help you plot all transformation activities related to a project in a visual format and be a repository for all project related materials (documents, drawings, checklists, contacts, communication, etc.). The level of complexity and cost varies from tool to tool. No matter which one you choose, it can help you keep all the balls in the air. Here's a list curated by The Digital Project manager: https://thedigitalprojectmanager.com/best-project-management-software/

Let's jump into this week's exercise.

Here's a simple project worksheet I've developed. Before you begin a project, I recommend you engage in, at least, this level of justification for the project. **(A version of this worksheet with full size blank lines is available on the companion website.)**

Project Title _____

Project Sponsor _____

Project Team _____

Project Cost: One-time _____

Ongoing _____

Reason:

Maintenance of Current Operations _____

Cost Saving _____

Increased Revenue _____

Compliance _____

Improved Customer Experience _____

Improved Employee Experience _____

If Increased Revenue or Cost Saving, what is the amount? _____

How does this project support the mission of the organization?

_____

Briefly describe the project

_____

What activities are required before the project begins (research, permits, etc.)?

_____

Project Plan

- Resources

  - People (employees, vendors, contractors, etc.)

  _____

  - Money (costs and payment schedule)

  _____

- Materials (materials to be transformed and materials needed for transformation activities)

  _____

- Timeline

  - Start date _____

  - Target completion date _____

  - Milestone events and dates _____

- Predecessor tasks and successor tasks (a successor task can also be a predecessor task for another activity)

  _____

- Possible impediments _____

- Training _____

- What does successful completion look like?_____

- How will progress be reported? _____

- To whom will progress be reported? _____

- Attach financial justification (e.g., payback, net present value, or internal rate of return)

Project Manager_____

Approved_____

During your exercise, review the available project management tools. Many include free trial periods, so for the first project scheduled after this One-Year, Thirty-Minute Business Transformation exercise, choose one or two that seem like a good fit for your organization and set up your project in both of those tools. Review the initial results with your project team and choose one and use it for the project.

Each project should have a project manager. This person's job is to be cheerleader, communicator, coordinator, butt-kicker, and problem solver. They should have a deep interest in the project itself and be able to articulate why it is important to the company. They should have not just the responsibility for the project, but also the authority to run the project team, manage project transformation activities, and spend from the project budget without being second-guessed.

The project manager should have a solid communication plan so that everyone on the team is always in sync and everyone else in the organization is up-to-date on the project's progress. Project status should be communicated to the team at least weekly and to the rest of the organization at least monthly.

The project manager's job is to drive the project to completion. When problems come, as they surely will, it is the project manager's job to make course corrections, marshal the resources of the team to resolve the problems, and refocus the team on project completion, all the while keeping the balls of time, materials, money, and people in the air.

After the end of every project, there should be a project postmortem where the project itself is evaluated, the project methodology is evaluated, and the project leader and team are evaluated. The goal of this postmortem is not to assign blame for anything that might have gone wrong but to refine the methodology and improve the team for the next project.

If you begin to build a project management framework using these initial guidelines, you'll be well on your way to effectively managing projects in your organization.

WEEK 32 :: LEADERSHIP :: ENVIRONMENT FOR GROWTH

If I'm listing the top five (maybe the top three) responsibilities of a leader, creating an environment that fosters growth absolutely makes the cut. An organization will most likely never grow beyond the person who leads it, and individual divisions and departments will most likely never grow beyond the people who lead them. Unfortunately, we human beings are wired for stasis. We run smack dab into Newton's first law of motion, "An object at rest stays at rest, and an object in motion stays in motion with the same speed and in the same direction unless acted upon by an external force." As a leader, it's your job to be that external force.

During this week's One-Year, Thirty-Minute Business Transformation exercise, I want to you to craft a framework that inspires and enables growth in your organization. The growth you want spans personal and professional, individual and team.

Use the ideas below like tools for your toolbox. Some, like the first one, I'd consider mandatory, and others might or might not work in your organization. Pick and choose, add your own, then execute. Make lifelong learning part of your organizational culture (*Learning Orientation* is in my list of cultural imperatives. If you want to see my full list of culture imperatives, you can find it in week twenty-six).

Set the Example for Personal and Professional Growth. You should be hearing phrases like this come out of your mouth frequently:

- "I was just reading…"

- "In the past, I would have…but with what I've learned now, I'd…"

- "I had to apologize for…because I found out I was wrong."

- "My gut feel was…but when I examined the data…"

- "Swing by my office because I'd like to get your thoughts on…"

Spend time reading, taking a class, listening to a TED talk, journaling, and writing.

Embrace and Communicate that "Ego is the Enemy." I've probably co-opted this title from Ryan Holiday's excellent book a thousand times as I've talked and written. However the real issue is whether or not I've embraced the message. We must never succumb to the temptation of thinking we know all there is to know about our job, our company, our customers, our people, or our processes. The minute we think we've arrived, the clock counting down our personal and professional destruction starts ticking. Advocate for personal and corporate humility. I often think about the encouragement from Gary Keller in his book *The One Thing*. We don't want to do our job the "best we can do it" (implying that our present capacity is the pinnacle). Instead, we want to do our job the "best it can be done" (implying that there's more to learn, and we're going to drink it all in and apply it in our work).

Create a Mentorship Program. Pair mentees with mentors who will talk with them about professional growth, career paths, navigating office politics, balancing work and family responsibilities, moving from staff to supervisory roles, and more. The mentor will learn just as much as the mentee. And you'll automatically be building a couple of the factors that employees identified as indicative of solid management (see *First, Break All the Rules* by Marcus

Buckingham). If potential mentors feel like this is outside their comfort zone, help them by creating a curriculum with discussion topics and resources.

Create an Environment where Good Risk is Embraced and Subsequent Failure after Good Risk is OK. If you never fail, you're more than likely never doing anything that's a stretch. People and organizations should do hard things. When the uncertainties surrounding hard things are pondered, good decision-making skills should be employed. Good decisions frequently result in bad outcomes (the batter swings at a pitch perfectly in the strike zone but hits a ground ball right at a player who fields the ball and turns a double play). If your good risk appears to end in failure, you've at least learned some things (faulty product development, faulty delivery, faulty messaging). It's never a bad thing to get an education.

Encourage Independent Work and Collaboration. Current research in productivity shows that neither bullpens nor private offices are optimal for the best outcomes. We need both. Employees need uninterrupted spans of time and privacy to do deep work (achieving flow). They also need engaging conversation with people who can challenge and sharpen the ideas they crafted working alone. Design workspaces and work schedules where both can happen.

Cross Discipline Knowledge is Golden. We have erroneously equated deep subject matter expertise with greater problem-solving ability in that discipline. For the sake of time, let me cut to the chase and say that thinking is wrong. In his book *Range*, David Epstein tells the story of two labs working on the same problem at the same time (proteins they wanted to measure would get stuck to a filter, which made them hard to analyze). One lab, staffed by only E. Coli experts, took weeks to solve the problem, experimenting with multiple methodologies. The other lab, staffed by scientists with chemistry, physics, biology, and genetics backgrounds, plus medical students, figured out the problem in their initial meeting. Deep subject matter expertise should be celebrated and leveraged, but to maximize peer-to-peer learning in an organization, utilize cross-disciplinary teams.

Make It Not All About Work. I know people who will come into an organization and do a Lunch-and-Learn session with topics like "Understanding Mortgages for First-Time Homebuyers," "Dog Training," "Personal Finances," and "Sleep." When your environment for growth includes growth opportunities for the whole person, you demonstrate another level of commitment to your team members.

Do the Traditional Stuff. Down through the years, employers have sent team members to seminars, enrolled them in online classes, and paid for college degrees. Some of these might make less sense now, but there's no reason to dismiss them entirely.

This is only a starter list, but it should get you on your way to creating a strong environment for growth in your organization.

WEEK 33 :: PEOPLE :: CORE VALUES

There has to be some mechanism by which employees gain admittance to your organization. Clearly, if you run a hospital and you need a thoracic surgeon, you're looking for someone with the right education, credentials, and experience. You employ a similar approach if you're hiring a plumber, chef, or accountant. But down through the years, hiring someone just because they have the right technical skills has resulted in a breathtakingly large number of terrible hires. "Qualified" hires have produced subpar work, destroyed morale, denigrated coworkers, undermined bosses, abused customers, and committed a truckload of other organizational "sins."

If technical skills are only one part of the screening process, what else should it include? In my opinion, you start with the Core Values of the organization. Core values are the personal and professional beliefs of the founder(s) that make their way into the behavior of the people in the organization. They're manifested in the priorities of the organization. They are the personal rules the founder(s) would live by no matter where they worked. They are the personal rules that the founder(s) would follow even if they became detrimental to the organization. They are the nonnegotiable ideals that govern interactions within the company (i.e., team member to team member), with customers, and with vendors. To borrow a phrase from the US founding documents, they are the truths that are self-evident. Employees who don't embrace and live out these values are destined to feel out of place in the organization.

Some things in an organization are a creative process—writing a mission statement, defining a vision, and, to a certain extent, even building a culture. But identifying core values is a discovery process.

When I do a core values exercise with a client, a few "values" surface immediately—honesty, integrity, and hardworking. I always make clients throw these out. These "price-of-admission" values don't count. No employer goes looking for employees who are dishonest, morally bankrupt, or lazy. The core values you're after are those four to eight overarching ideas that make up your organization's behavioral compass.

I'm always reluctant to use my company to illustrate a point, but in this case, it might make sense. Here are three of the core values of ClearVision Consulting:

- *A love for small-business owners.* I hold in the highest regard those people who have risked their personal wealth and banked on their God-given talent to uniquely solve problems for their target clients. Their desire to build a better life for themselves and their families must be celebrated. They deserve to have someone in their corner equipping them and cheering them on.

- *A desire to dig deep and understand the client's business.* I will learn as much about the client's business as they will allow me to learn. Over the years, as I've done research into process improvements or created strategic plans, I've loaded produce on a truck, checked in resort guests, stocked shelves in a store, sat in board meetings and staff meetings, conducted interviews, evaluated vendors, written SQL code, and a few hundred more things. More times than I can count, I've fielded calls from executives who had questions about how things work inside their organizations, and I've been able to answer them because I'm intimately familiar with their work. If I don't know the client's company intimately, how can I help them craft strategies that will take them where they want to go and remake processes that will transform their value-creation activities?

- *A commitment to treat client resources like they are my own.* Before I recommend that a client spend money, hire or fire an employee, or invest in a new product or market, I ask myself if I'd make the same investment with my own resources. They deserve someone who will preserve their hard-fought-for capital.

If someone came to work with me and didn't hold to these values, they'd never survive in the organization. This is who I am, and, as far as I'm concerned, this is how business should be done. This is the way core values work. They are heartfelt beliefs that translate into real-life actions in the organization.

Before we jump into this week's exercise, let me remind you how you're going to use your core values. I used employment as my opening example, and that will be an important application, but you want to use your core values to judge *all* future associations. If you use vendors who share your core values, they become true partners. If you market to customers who share your core values, they become strong referrals partners for you and might even give you a couple of mulligans if you drop the ball.

So how do you find the core values of your organization? The answers to these questions should get you there.

- What business behavior makes you mad when you see it? Why does it make you mad? Which of your closely held values is "offended"?

- What are the worst ways your employees could drop the ball? What could they do that would ruin your company's reputation? Lose customers? Make you feel ashamed of the company? Which of your closely held beliefs about how to do business are being violated?

- If you worked for another company, what personal rules would you live by (taking care of customers, looking out for the company's equipment, etc.) even if the company's rules were less stringent?

- What behaviors would you maintain even if it were detrimental to the company financially?

- What behaviors do you admire in other people and companies and seek to emulate? Why?

- When customers speak favorably about your company, what qualities do they cite? What did you or your employees do to make them get that vibe?

- What are the jointly revered business beliefs and behaviors in the core team (the people who've stuck around the longest and who constitute the DNA of the company)? What makes them stay and stay loyal?

Get answers to these questions down on paper or a whiteboard and connect some dots. What themes surface? Look for approaches to work (e.g., data-driven decision-making or brutal honesty among team members), approaches to customers (e.g., highly tailored solutions or first-call problem resolution), and operational priorities (e.g., work products that don't require rework or open book management). Select four to eight and include a short description with each one. Here are a couple of examples:

- *Balance*: We control our schedule and successfully manage our personal and professional priorities and accord that privilege and the trust that goes with it to everyone in the organization.

- *Rewarding*: Our work brings exceptional value to the client and enriches us personally and professionally.

Roll your list out to a few folks in the organization. Ask them, "Is this us?" If they say, "No," ask them why not. That might indicate that you, as a leader, aren't living out your values in the organization. Take their feedback and return to the drawing board. Repeat until you've got your final list.

After you have it, write questions to use in your interview process that help job candidates explain how they embody these values. If they don't have the values, don't hire them. Then, use the values to vet vendors and write marketing content. You're looking for people who, as Simon Sinek would say, "share your why."

WEEK 34 :: STRATEGIC PLANNING :: CREATIVE DESTRUCTION

Someone else would like to take your customers. Any time an industry, company, product, or service attracts a crowd (and the revenue that crowd generates), there will be a host of fast followers who show up and try to siphon off some of that revenue for themselves or try to grow the size of the market, so they can have a piece of the market share and revenue.

Those fast followers have a few options—create a better version of the original product or service, create a cheaper version of the product or service, create a product or service that is complementary to the original product or service, or *re-solve the original problem in a radically different way, rendering the original product or service obsolete.*

Let's illustrate with personally curated portable music. For years, portable music took the form of radio. Other than choosing a station that played the genre of music you liked, you were unable to curate your own listening. Then, in the mid-1960s, Bill Lear (of Learjet fame) invented the eight-track tape player; I had one in my first two cars. You were able to choose albums produced by your favorite artists. It was subsequently replaced by cassettes (again complete albums), then CDs (still complete albums), then downloadable digital songs (on iPods and similar MP3 devices), and now streaming online music (both of the latest two offer choices of mingling genres, albums, and individual songs). Each of these successor technologies destroyed the commercial viability of the previous technology. Companies that failed to embrace the successor technology became irrelevant and, in some cases, closed their doors.

Recent history is loaded with companies that failed to reinvent their value-creation proposition and paid the price: Blockbuster, Kodak, Polaroid, Myspace, Yahoo, and Blackberry, just to name a few. These all have a tech component, but there are plenty of non-tech-related companies that have failed to remake their value-creation activities. Toys "R" Us, Sears, Radio Shack, Borders, and Circuit City are among them.

Joseph Schumpeter popularized the term "creative destruction" in his 1942 book *Capitalism, Socialism, and Democracy*. According to Schumpeter, the "gale of creative destruction" is the "process of industrial mutation that continuously revolutionizes the economic structure from within, incessantly destroying the old one, incessantly creating a new one." This is what makes capitalism an engine for creating wealth for those who identify a problem and find a commercially viable solution to that problem. At the very same time, those who cling to solutions that are no longer commercially viable will find their ability to create wealth wiped out.

Let's jump into this week's One-Year, Minute Business Transformation. I have three goals for this week's exercise:

- I want you to examine your value-creation activities for your existing products or services.

- I want you to ponder successor products for your existing products or services.

- I want you to examine the competitive landscape for someone who is introducing a product or service that poses a threat to your existing products or services.

Value Creation for your Existing Product or Service

Your existing product or service might be in demand and effectively solving a customer's problem. That's great. But what if a competitor could introduce a similar product but at half the price due to a new manufacturing technology? Not all creative destruction means retiring or remaking an existing product or service. It might mean destroying and remaking the methodology for creating or delivering your product. Are there new technologies, new contract manufacturers, new materials, or even streamlined processes that would allow you to manufacture your product or service faster, with higher quality, or cheaper? Are there new delivery channels or options that would allow you to get your product or service in the customer's hands faster, cheaper, or with a better customer experience?

Successor Products or Services

When you're pondering creative destruction, the goal is not always a better mouse trap. Before cars were introduced, people just wanted faster horses. They never envisioned a "horseless carriage." You're after a better solution to the problem you're solving for your customers—think digital camera vs. traditional film or Netflix vs. Blockbuster. Is there a better way to solve the same problem for your customers? Can you piggyback on other infrastructures or technologies? Can you partner with another company to create something that neither company could do on their own? Is there a methodology from another industry that's never been used in your industry but could be leveraged to solve your customer's problem?

Surveying the Competitive Landscape

The worst place to be in the world of creative destruction is behind the curve. Someone else has already solved your customer's problem in a better way, and they're already eating into your customer base. The early adopters have switched to the competitor's product or service, and it appears to be going well. One quick warning: the scrapheap of failed businesses is primarily populated by companies who got to this point and stuck their head in the sand with thoughts like, "Nobody wants a computer in their house," "The internet is just a fad," and "People want real pictures they can hold in their hands." Don't be that company. Take competitive threats seriously. So what do you do as you survey the landscape? If you're still strong and the successor product is just getting out of the gate, the company that produces it might be an acquisition target. In the right circumstances, you might be able to buy them outright. If they're undercapitalized, they might need some cash to grow, and you might be able to buy a significant stake and ride the elevator up with them. In other cases, you might be able to create a competitive product and leverage your brand, bigger war chest, and existing customer base to beat back the new entrant.

The big idea in this week's exercise is to never be lulled into complacency. Great companies earn it every time they go into the marketplace. They reexamine their products, services, and delivery methodologies to make sure they are always solving the customer's problem in the best way possible.

WEEK 35 :: FINANCE :: CAPITAL BUDGETING

It's that time of year when companies look at their Capital Budgets for the upcoming year. Capital budgets differ from operating budgets in a couple of important ways. Capital budgets represent a trade, swapping one type of asset for another—$30,000 in cash for a $30,000 delivery truck or $100,000 in cash for a $100,000 enterprise software package. These capital purchases are reflected only on the Balance Sheet. Later, they make their way to the Income Statement and Balance Sheet a chunk at a time using an accounting mechanism called *depreciation*. Depreciation is driven by the "class life" for each capital purchase. At the time this chapter is being written (August 2020), IRS guidelines set the class life for real property at thirty-nine years, office furniture at seven years, and autos and trucks at five years. So for our $30,000 delivery truck example earlier in the paragraph, we're spending the physical $30,000 in cash now and reflecting the purchase only on the Balance Sheet – the cash comes off, and the truck goes on. Going forward, we're going to recognize the depreciation on both the Income Statement and the Balance Sheet. Each year, for the first five years we own the truck, we'll see $6,000 of depreciation expense on the Income Statement and $6,000 removed from the value of the truck on the Balance Sheet; in actuality, on the Balance Sheet, the depreciation will be accumulated in a single account with all the rest of the depreciation. Conversely, operating budgets are for those expenses that don't represent a "swap" of assets. Salaries, utilities, and every other noncapital expense happen here. The accounting piece is very simple—reduce cash (on the Balance Sheet) and recognize the expense (on the Income Statement).

The goal of this week's One-Year, Minute Business Transformation is to begin building a capital budgeting process that you can use this year and sharpen in the upcoming years. Keep using it and refining it, so it always serves your organization well. Here's a high-level outline. Your job is to flesh out the steps and fit it to your organization.

Let's jump in.

Identify Potential Capital Budget Items. The company's strategic direction and operational necessities should drive this part of the exercise. Typically, there's no shortage of items clamoring for your capital expense dollars. You might want to enter a new, promising market that requires a new office, new equipment, or new vehicles. You might have to replace worn-out factory machinery or desktop computers to continue existing operations. You might need new equipment to comply with recently mandated government environmental regulations. You might be able to lower manufacturing costs by capitalizing on a new process, but it requires retooling the factory.

Estimate the Financial Impact of the Proposed Capital Budget Items. Using the best information you can gather from vendors, sales, operations, and finance experts, determine the financial effect of the proposed projects on your organization. What will the item(s) cost to obtain? What will the item(s) cost to operate in the first year and all subsequent years? What additional revenue will the item(s) generate in the first year and all subsequent years? If the items are available from multiple vendors, compare item features, benefits, costs, and expected revenues for each option.

Evaluate the Proposed Items and their Financial Performance. Typically, you'll begin your capital budgeting process with a pool of money you're ready to devote to capital projects. After you've gathered all the information during the previous step, you're ready to evaluate the proposed projects, hopefully using more science than art. Regulatory compliance gets first dibs since failure to comply could put the ongoing operation of the business in jeopardy. The remainder of the projects should be evaluated by the finance folks using some tried and true capital budgeting metrics that we'll discuss shortly, but a couple of things first. In many cases, the money to be spent will come from cash on hand. That money isn't free. If it sat in an interest-bearing investment, it would have a return. For purposes of discussion, let's say the return on the cash on hand, if left in the investment, is 3 percent. The return on investment for the proposed capital project needs to be more than 3 percent. If the money for the capital project is going to be borrowed at an interest rate of 5 percent, the return on investment for the proposed capital project needs to be more than 5 percent. You get the idea—the return on the project needs to be more financially beneficial than doing nothing. Clearly, regulatory capital expenses get a mulligan here. There may be no financial benefit to the project. In fact, there might be only financial detriment. But most likely, the financial detriment is far less than the impact of closing the company. In these cases, the increased costs must be passed along to consumers or be borne by stockholders in the form of lower profits.

Let's talk about five of the most commonly employed methodologies for evaluating capital projects:

- *Payback Period.* How quickly will the cash inflows generated by the investment pay back the initial investment? If the initial investment is $10,000 and the investment generates $5,000 a year in additional cash, the payback period is two years. This method is quick and simple, but it doesn't take into account the value of cash inflows after the payback period or the time value of money.

- *Net Present Value (NPV).* This methodology compares the present value of all future cash inflows resulting from the project to the present value of all the current and future outflows required to execute the project.

- *Profitability Index.* The present value of all future cash inflows associated with the project divided by the present value of the current and future cash outflows associated with the project.

- *Internal Rate of Return (IRR).* This methodology identifies the rate at which the project breaks even by examining the cash inflows and outflows.

- *Modified Internal Rate of Return (MIRR).* This methodology is similar to the IRR except that it recognizes that cash inflows can be reinvested at a rate that is different than the rate at which they were generated.

Each of the capital projects under consideration must be evaluated in light of these financial metrics (and possibly others). The purpose of this week's exercise is not to get deeply in the woods, but there are always additional considerations like tax consequence and accounting methodologies. Your finance folks can guide you into a complete discussion.

Most years, you'll have more potential projects than you have money. The objective measures above will help the projects with the highest return on investment (ROI) bubble to the top.

Occasionally, you'll be choosing between proposed projects with similar returns, sometimes offering mutually exclusive options. At that point, the "art" kicks in. The projects that most successfully move your strategy forward, the influence of nonfinancial data (market sizes, trends, patterns, etc.), management knowledge and intuition, and more will inform your decision on which projects to pick and which projects to reject or defer.

Implement. After the winning projects are selected, execute like crazy. Depending on the type of project, you might need to create a project team (hope you included that in your capital budget). Create schedules with timelines and milestones, align vendor resources, employ a solid execution framework, and communicate well. You want to implement the project as quickly as possible so it can start generating the cash inflows.

Measure. The capital budgeting tools were forward-looking. After implementation, rigorously track the actual results. Hopefully the project is performing better than you projected. However, one of the worst mistakes a company can make is succumbing to "sunk cost fallacy." If a project is seriously underperforming, and there's no remedy in sight, it's noble to pull the plug. The fact that you've already spend $50,000 or $5,000,000 becomes immaterial. Continually investing resources with the hope that the project will magically turn around is a mistake rooted in pride. Track the performance of each project, so you have better information for your next round of capital budgeting.

Capital budgeting, many times, represents an opportunity to make a big leap for an organization. A new market, product, process, or system can catapult a company into the national spotlight or into a level of revenue never even dreamed of before. Take this exercise seriously.

WEEK 36 :: TECHNOLOGY :: BIG DATA

According to Statista, in 2010, the total of amount of data collected world-wide was two zettabytes. Or to use a unit of measurement you might be more familiar with, that's two trillion gigabytes. In 2024, that number is projected to hit 149 zettabytes. All that data isn't kept, so IDC predicts that by 2025, the world's accumulated datastore will be 175 zettabytes. According to Forbes, we (collectively) generate 1.7 megabytes of new data per person per second. And here's maybe the most interesting fact of all: according to IDC, less than 5 percent of that data will be analyzed.

Why is any of that important in the world of the One-Year, Thirty-Minute Business Transformation? Because companies who capitalize on the data available to their organization are seeing results. They are

- identifying what parts of that data directly impact their financial performance,

- making meaning of that data with expert analysis,

- turning that analysis into actionable insights,

- changing organizational behavior based on those insights,

- measuring the financial impact of those changes,

- and making additional changes based on those measurements.

Here are a few examples from Tech Republic.

- Supply chain safety and theft detection enables companies, with help of item-placed sensors and business intelligence, to reduce in-transit theft rates of supplies from 50 percent to 4 percent and to detect when the environmental controls or seals on shipment containers have been compromised.

- Logistics tracking and routing using business intelligence and machine-based data/sensors optimize delivery routes and driver habits, creating fuel savings and better service.

- Collections work at companies is avoided by learning more about customers who are behind on their payments through big data aggregation and business intelligence that can predict who in good faith can pay their debts with a little help. Companies can then help these customers keep their purchases and keep themselves from having to write off defaults.

- Buying habits and preferences of consumers are better understood and lead to increased sales.

- Predictive maintenance enables urban tram systems to stay online, reroute traffic where necessary, and flash adviser alerts to customers over their mobile phones while repair crews are dispatched to replace faulty components before the components actually fail.

Big Data doesn't just refer to just the volume of data available today; it encompasses the "four V's" of big data":

- **Volume**. Certainly, volume is an important part of the equation. We have internal data from our CRM and ERP systems that tell us about vendor performance, product performance, customer behavior, employee performance, and a host of other things. We have external data from social networks, online review sites, and more. Because of the *Internet of Things (IoT)*, we have data that originates not just from the actions of our employees or customers but from inanimate devices connected to the internet. So we can know the number of times a door opens and for whom, the temperature inside a shipping container, and when a client's copier is low on toner.

- **Variety.** This data comes at us in multiple ways: structured data from internal systems where we've controlled what is collected (and how) and unstructured data from external sources. We might get a text from a customer with a video of the dishwasher we just fixed showing us that it's still doing what it was doing before we "fixed" it, a Google review, a Twitter DM, a reading from a sensor on our delivery van alerting us to a tire pressure problem, and the list goes on.

- **Velocity.** If the previous two aren't enough, maybe the most daunting is the speed at which it comes at us. Last minute's data reporting that all is well is superseded by this minute's data reporting a problem on the factory floor or a customer unhappy with your product or service. Multiply those by the number of inputs (customers, employees, vendors, and sensors), and it can seem overwhelming.

- **Value.** In actuality, this is the one that matters most. Of all the data collected by your organization, what really impacts financial performance, customer experience, and employee well-being (their ability to do their job effectively and efficiently)?

One more thing before we jump into this week's exercise. Big Data requires different skills and tools than the traditional reporting you've pulled from your internal systems. First, because of the mix of structured and unstructured data, you'll need a data management infrastructure that can manage both. Second, you need someone who can help you navigate this new world. You can hire a data scientist, or you might opt for outsourcing this part of your work to a vendor specializing in big data analysis. The most rudimentary big data analyses are looking for trends (e.g., Each month for the past six months, distributors of our product in the Southeast have reported a stock out. Each month, it's been earlier in the month than the month before), patterns (customers whose first purchase from us is product X never make another purchase, but customers whose first purchase is product Y have an 80 percent chance of being a repeat customer), and correlations (in the fall, the first time the temperature dips below fifty degrees, canned soup sales double and stay at that level until the first time the temperature hits sixty degrees in the Spring). A Data Scientist can help you start thinking in this vein. Third, in addition to the infrastructure tools to do the heavy lifting, you need visualization tools that help you easily see what this large amount of data is telling you. Even if the data scientist tells you everything you need to know, you want to roll this information out to everyone in the organization who can benefit from it. Good visualization tools will allow them to consume large amounts of information (and make sense of it) more easily.

For this week's exercise, I want you to identify some problems or opportunities in the organization where big data-generated insights might make a difference. Here are some thought starters:

- *More callbacks on service calls.* Is it the same technician? Are they working on the same brand of equipment? Are replacement parts from the same vendor failing at a high rate?

- *Inventory management is more challenging than it should be.* Can you get access to distributor data, so you can see when distributors are most likely to place a reorder? Is a single vendor slowing production with late or defective products?

- *Customers seem uninterested in a new product or service.* What is the factory defect rate on this product vs. the defect rate on its predecessor? Have customers who purchased the product commented on social media regarding the product? Is it especially unpopular among your customers who purchase another product from you?

- *We have too many employees during some shifts and not enough during others.* Can you examine sales per hour for the same day of the week last week or the same week last year? Can you examine the nature of sales during each shift, that is, selling a hand-dipped ice cream cone is more labor-intensive than selling a bottled soft drink?

Take your list and contact a big data company for a consultation. See if it makes sense to do a pilot project.

Big data is the foundation for technologies like *Machine Learning,* the improvement of computer algorithms through experience (e.g., people who bought this book also bought this book, powering your Amazon recommendations), and Artificial Intelligence, when a system "perceives its environment and takes actions that maximize its chance of successfully achieving its goals" (think Big Blue playing chess against a Grand Master, examining the chess board and making the optimal chess move).

Of all the technology assets in your company, data is the most important. It catalogs the past behavior of your employees and customers, and, lest we forget, the best predictor of future behavior is past behavior. Don't neglect the power of this asset to solve problems that have puzzled you for a long time.

WEEK 37 :: STRATEGIC PLANNING :: BULLETS, THEN CANNONBALLS

In his 2011 book, *Great by Choice,* Jim Collins introduced the concept of "Fire Bullets, Then Cannonballs." Create a low-cost, low-risk product or service launch (a bullet) and measure its success. If the bullet came close to the target (good consumer appeal, more profitable, potential to capture more share, etc.), recalibrate (refine the offering, improve the delivery, hone the messaging, etc.) and fire again. In the course of this iterative process, when the bullet hits the bullseye (confirmed by data), invest in the proven offering and craft a fully developed product or service paired with a strong launch (a cannonball).

It's easy for a person or an organization to become enamored with an unproven "cannonball" that's going to propel the organization to the front of their industry (or create a new industry) and cause their revenue and profits to soar. We love the idea, and our ego convinces us that we've found a unicorn. To be sure, those cannonballs are out there, but, compared to the number of companies and product launches, those products or services are, as they say, scarcer than hen's teeth. Plenty of companies have lost money (and investor's money) by shooting unproven cannonballs from the beginning without any evidence they would find the bullseye. For most of us mortals, the path to sustained competitive advantage is bullets first then cannonballs.

In this week's One-Year, Thirty-Minute Business Transformation, I want you to spend your exercise identifying opportunities in your organization where you can craft some bullets. Take these six "bullet starters," get your team together, and take a virtual walk through your organization. See how many bullet opportunities you can identify.

- **Create a Pilot Product from Scratch.** Over the last few years, software companies have taught us the value of creating a *Minimum Viable Product (MVP)*. For example, early versions of Gmail, Evernote, and Google Docs had only a fraction of the features they have now. That's because the purpose of the early versions was to gauge interest and commercial viability. When it became clear that the products had potential, only then was more development effort expended to make a full-featured product (and the development goes on today). Can you create a minimum viable product to explore a new market or a new segment within an existing market?

- **Change the Customer Experience.** Could you increase conversion rates for new customers, increase retention rates for existing customers, or streamline internal operations by changing the customer experience? Maybe you could deliver food to tables instead of calling a number or change the automated call routing on your phone system, making it easier for a customer to talk to a live person. Make small, measurable changes, survey customers to get their feedback, and track the financial impact. If customers respond favorably, continue to tweak the customer experience until customers experience function, form, and feeling when interacting with your organization.

- **Create a Stripped-Down Version of an Existing Product.** One of the things we hopefully learned from the coronavirus crisis was the ability to pivot. If our successful, three-day, on-site training program isn't an option, what do we do to make money? Strip out one of the topics from one of the days and create a webinar. It sells for a fraction of the price and customers can consume it from their home. Look for the opportunity to deconstruct an existing product or service and sell a stripped-down or fractional version. You might find that smaller micro-offerings are more profitable and have the added advantage of opening the door for larger sales later.

- **Create Another Product from an Existing Product.** Many years ago, back when I had a corporate job, one of the smartest things I ever saw my former employer do was take something worthless and make it into something valuable. In their heyday, newspapers accumulated thousands of pictures each year. Only a small fraction of those ever made it into the newspaper. So what do you do with all those unused pictures? My former employer made them into coffee table books. They identified several themes—architecture, sports, and signs to name a few—combed through decades of pictures and put together fascinating collections of photos in very cool coffee table books. What assets do you have that you could recompile into a new product or service?

- **Develop a Strategic Partnership.** If you run a service company—an exterminator, for example—could you begin to offer wildlife removal services to your customers by partnering with an existing wildlife removal service? This type of relationship allows you to "stick your toe in the water" with very little downside risk. If the test goes well, you might consider a merger or acquisition, or you might add that expertise to your staff and expand your service offerings.

- **Tap the Collective Genius of your Team.** For years, 3M operated with the "30 Percent Rule"—Thirty percent of revenue had to come from products created in the previous four years. To fuel that initiative, 3M authorized "15 percent time"—Fifteen percent of an employee's work week could be devoted to projects that were interesting to them, not mandated by their boss. Post-It Notes and light-recycling lens (a $100 million product) came from 15 percent time. Google, for a while, crafted their own version (in their case 20 percent time). Gmail, AdSense, Google Maps, and Google Talk were born from 20 percent time. I'm not saying you need to give employees one day per week to do what is interesting to them, but I am saying there are ideas ruminating in the minds of your employees. You need to create a mechanism to get them out. Fund some pilot projects that come from employees. You might find a future cannonball.

Here's a quick primer as you begin your exercise:

- **Use speed as a differentiator.** Make a product variation where the price is cheaper but delivery is slower or make a product variation where the price is higher and delivery is faster.

- **Use geography.** Limit the reach of your bullet. If you're going to start delivery, do it in a small radius. If you're going to introduce a new product, only offer it in one of your locations.

- **Remove risk.** Use a freemium/premium model—a stripped-down version for free or a version with more features for a fee.

- **Build testing into the bullet launch.** Take advantage of A/B testing. You can keep an existing product or customer experience for a control group, then offer your "bullet" offering in another group. Or you can make a couple of similar bullet products (or messaging options) and launch them together. Track them side-by-side. If your bullet offering is sold online, there are dozens of tools that will facilitate this.

Select two or three bullet opportunities from your list, recruit a project sponsor from your team for each of the bullet opportunities, create the bullets, and launch them. Measure demand and solicit feedback. Be brave enough to kill the bullets that are too far from the bullseye, then be relentless iteratively honing and relaunching those that show promise, eventually crafting cannonballs.

WEEK 38 :: OPERATIONS :: CUSTOMER ONBOARDING

There's nothing more critical to a great customer experience than onboarding. Many times, we limit "onboarding" to something we do with a new employee, but every stakeholder in the organization should have an onboarding experience. Onboarding sets expectations, defines responsibilities and describes "winning."

In this week's One-Year, Thirty-Minute Business Transformation, we're focusing on *Customer Onboarding*, but many of the outcomes and methodologies can be applied to other stakeholder groups.

Here's why onboarding is so important. Have you ever received a movie recommendation from a trusted friend and, after watching the movie, realized you'd never get those two wasted hours of your life back (or in the case of *Dances with Wolves*, four hours)? It's pretty disappointing. But why is it disappointing? Because the friend's glowing recommendation created *high expectations*. In the absence of that recommendation, you might have still hated the movie, but you would have just added it to the list of movies you'll never watch again. But now, you're presented with confusion. You've had reliable recommendations from that friend in the past. What did you miss in the movie that your friend loved? How are you going to explain your disappointment to your friend? Will you ever be able to trust their recommendations in the future?

This all stems from faulty expectations created at the beginning of the interaction. We can have the same problem when we begin a relationship with a new customer. If we don't successfully create correct expectations at the beginning of a relationship, the customer will create their own. Those will come from experience ("The last time I hired a plumber, it took them an hour to replace my kitchen faucet"), from hope ("I would love it if the plumber spread a tarp in front of the sink before they began working on the drain") and from people who influence them ("My friend hired a plumber, and it cost them $300 to get their sink unclogged").

Let's jump into this week's exercise. We want to finish with a rock-solid customer onboarding framework. Depending on your product or service, this could be very simple or a bit complex. You can do this one solo or invite some trusted team members who are familiar with the flow of work from initial customer contact to delivery. We're going to focus our attention on three things—*expectations*, *responsibilities*, and *metrics*.

Before I jump into the steps below, let me quickly say that I'm aware we're talking about a mix of communication, some before the sale and some after the sale. I realize that in some presale messaging, you're selling a feeling or experience (e.g., someone buying insurance is buying peace of mind in the midst of an unfortunate circumstance, not a policy). The bulk of the ideas below are to create clarity of expectation, responsibility, and metrics. You decide where to deliver them in your messaging based on your product, service, and desired delivery experience.

Expectations

- *Succinctly describe what product or service the customer is buying.* A great meal at a great price. The most sophisticated timepiece you'll ever own. You'll never know your car was wrecked.

- *Give clear direction to the first step in the discovery or purchase process.* Visit our showroom at 123 Main Street. Contact one of our friendly customer service representatives at 555-555-5555. Click here to schedule an initial appointment.

- *Explain the steps in which you create value for the customer.* It all starts with a free health assessment; in less than an hour, we'll email you the results of the assessment along with our recommendations; in three days we'll contact you and get your decision on which weight loss program is best for you; we'll kick off your exercise and diet plan, and by week four, you'll be down ten pounds.

- *Explain what interactions will look like.* You'll never be stuck in voicemail jail—a real person will always answer the phone. You'll be able to manage your account from anywhere on our award-winning mobile app. You'll have unlimited support via email with a four-hour guaranteed response time.

- *If your product or service has inherent uncertainty, explain the path from uncertainty to certainty.* When our technician arrives to examine your appliance, you'll get a full explanation of the problem and a complete estimate of what it will cost to fix it; we'll get your OK before we proceed with any repair; when it's fixed, the parts and labor are guaranteed for one year.

- *Explain the customer's financial responsibility.* The cost will be $99 per month for the first six months, then $129 per month for thirty-three months. There's a $400 administrative fee on top of the price of the car. (If you want to make customers extremely unhappy, bury some previously undisclosed cost in the fine print.)

- *Explain what will happen if something goes wrong.* Our workmanship is guaranteed for ten years. If your roof leaks, we'll fix it at no charge to you. This is the best snow cone you've ever eaten or your money back. If you don't like the like the paint color you've chosen with our patented color match system, we'll repaint your room for free.

Responsibilities

One of the key parts of customer onboarding is explaining the customer's role in the delivery of your product or service.

- *Define deadlines.* For your policy to be in effect by October 11, 2020, we need your driver's license number and the VIN from your car by September 30, 2020. To terminate your lease, please notify us 180 days before the renewal date.

- *Explain their involvement.* The number of used treadmills, ellipticals, and Chuck Norris Total Gyms on Craigslist owned by people who are still overweight are a testament to the number of customers who don't embrace their responsibility during onboarding. Customers buy, what appear to be, solutions to a problem they are experiencing. Clearly lay out the steps they must take for that problem to be resolved. And explain the how not just the what.

- *Provide engagement tools.* Think about the number of companion apps you have for the products or services you consume. I can lower my thermostat, manage my robot vacuum, change the payment method for my car insurance, and get a reminder when my Home Depot credit card bill is due on my phone. Each time you make it easier to interact with your product or service, you help the customer derive more value from the product or service, make it easier for the customer to fulfill their responsibilities, and ultimately solve their problem. Engagement tools don't have to be as sophisticated as a mobile app. I recently got a bid from a roofing company to replace my roof. Part of their proposal was a checklist for me to follow before they began work on my home. The checklist explained not only what I needed to do but why it would aid them in quickly solving my problem—getting a new roof on my house in the minimum amount of time and with the least amount of expense.

- *Give examples of customers who have successfully engaged the product or service and achieved the desired results.* These examples inspire, inform, and help customers connect the dots between what the product does and what they must do.

Metrics

Everyone wants to "win" with their purchase. In the onboarding experience, we need to accurately identify winning for them.

- *Help customers measure leading indicators not just trailing indicators.* If they buy exercise equipment, "winning" is working out twenty minutes a day and cutting their caloric intake, not losing twenty pounds. If they do the former, they will get the latter.

- *Help customers attach greater meaning to their purchases.* The financial planner's 1 percent annual management fee isn't a cost; it's an investment in someone who devotes their professional life to helping clients secure their financial future and the financial future of the client's family.

- *Help customers attach greater reach to their purchases.* The business coaching purchased by the CEO doesn't just benefit the executive. As they become a more effective leader and push what they learn down through the organization, all who work for that executive benefit. And, by increasing the organization's effectiveness and efficiency, shareholders benefit.

When expectations, responsibilities, and metrics are clearly defined for a new customer, everyone involved in the equation knows how to behave. If the company fails to deliver on the expectations, they can quickly make it right. If the customer fails to live up to their obligations, the company can jump in with a bit of accountability and encouragement to get the relationship back on track. When both parties agree on what "winning" looks like, they can track it with reporting and reinforce it with messaging.

WEEK 39 :: STRATEGIC PLANNING :: ANNUAL PLAN

Strategic Plans fail at an alarming rate. According to *The Balanced Scorecard*, 90 percent of businesses fail to execute their strategies successfully. According to *onstrategyhq.com*, 95 percent of employees don't understand their organization's Strategic Plan, and 60 percent of companies don't link strategy to budget. If those are the stats, why even engage in the strategic planning process at all?

First, there's value in the process. General, and later President, Dwight Eisenhower said, "In preparing for battle, I have always found that plans are useless, but planning is indispensable." Every plan, whether it's for a military campaign or for running a donut shop, is built on informed theory and assumptions. But the minute those plans are implemented, they become vulnerable to forces outside our control. The enemy has more artillery than we anticipated. The muffin shop down the street lowers their prices. Does that mean it's time to abandon our plan? That all our planning effort was wasted? No, it means just the opposite. If we exercised the discipline to plan thoroughly, we contemplated multiple actions and the anticipated outcomes for each. We chose one, or possibly a couple, of those actions and assembled the resources to execute it. But the real value in planning was that we analyzed all of the possible actions, all of the possible outcomes, and all of the resources necessary to execute those actions. Now, this knowledge is at our disposal. So when reality collides with our plan, and our initial choices don't seem so wise, we already have a wealth of accumulated thought on how to readjust and redeploy our resources to still achieve our original objective.

Second, there's value in the discipline. It is very easy to be caught in the tyranny of the urgent. Crises with employees, customers, vendors, equipment, and money can consume every waking work minute. Dedicating time for deliberate planning gets us off the hamster wheel of constant busyness. The discipline of

- thoughtfully examining our *human resources*, the people we have now and the people we'll need in the future;

- carefully evaluating our *value-creation activities*—supply chain, transformation activities, and vendor performance;

- revisiting our *financial management*—liquidity, cash management, and return on invested capital;

- carefully considering our *market*—customer problems we are solving, messaging, and competitors;

- and taking the temperature of our organization—culture and metrics

helps us see things clearly and truthfully with fresh eyes and helps us more accurately plot a new course that moves us closer to our vision for the organization.

The biggest reason that strategic plans fail is lack of execution. Execution must be baked into the plan from the beginning and pursued fanatically through the entire organization as the plan is rolled out. A good strategic planning methodology leans heavily to the implementation side.

Let's jump into this week's One-Year, Thirty-Minute Business Transformation. Clearly you won't finish your thirty-minute exercise with a strategic plan, but that's not the goal. The goal for this week's exercise is to identify the people who will be involved, set up a time, and decide on a process.

- **Good strategic plans require input from up and down the food chain.** The larger the organization, the more difficult this becomes. As organizations grow, people at the top necessarily move away from important value-creation activities and customer interactions. But those are the very activities and interactions that must inform future strategic plans. The first order of business is making sure that all the information you need to get an accurate picture of the current state of your organization is in the room. Gathering that information and involving people in the strategic planning process who can accurately interpret and advocate for the stakeholder interests represented by that information is crucial.

- **Put it on the calendar and don't let anything displace it.** Find a time and make it happen. Depending on the size of your organization and how solidly your mission, vision, and core values are defined, it might take a day, or it might take a week. If you've spent time on carefully defining your mission and vision, and you are solid on your core values, you can jump straight into your strategic planning exercise. If those things are new to you, you'll want to spend time on those first. For a frame of reference, when I'm doing a strategic planning workshop with a client ($20 million or less in annual revenue), we spend at least three full days or six half-days working together (that includes working on the mission, vision, and core values). If we determine the current state of the organization is far from the future state the leaders want, we might spend a couple of extra days hammering out the first steps in the desired transformation and the methodology we'll employ to implement those steps. Once you've put the planning exercise on the calendar, make sure you protect the time both for yourself and for those working with you on the plan.

- **Decide on a process.** There are a number of good strategic planning processes and tools out there. They range from the one-page variety to more complete and detailed frameworks. Remember, much of the value is in the discipline of the exercise, so no matter the framework, utilize fully, think deeply, and create deliberately. Here are the things you want to look for in whatever framework you use.

— **Get an accurate picture of the current state of your organization.** One of the most frequent and most damaging mistakes in a strategic planning exercise is failing to get an accurate picture of where you are now as an organization. You spend a lot of time on where you want to go but not nearly enough on where you are now. How can you make a map from here to there unless know your current location? Find a framework with powerful assessment tools.

— **Create several fully loaded future scenarios.** With your knowledge of the current state of your organization, your assessment of your place in the external environment (with customers, competitors, and regulators) and the efficacy of your products or services to successfully solve problems for current and potential customers, craft a number of strategic alternatives. These alternatives might solve a personnel problem, correct an operational deficiency, exploit a market opportunity, recreate an existing product or service, or tech-enable your customer experience. Some alternatives might play well with others. Some might be bold and very different from what you're doing now.

— **Evaluate and choose the best opportunities.** Your framework should give you tools to evaluate your alternatives in the light of financial return on investment (i.e., measuring the impact on shareholders in the long-term and in the short-term). You should also evaluate your alternatives considering employee experience, customer experience, regulatory compliance, and, of course, in how much the alternative will push your organization closer to your vision. This part of the exercise should yield three, or at the most four, initiatives that you'll be implementing over the next twelve to eighteen months.

— **Execute like crazy.** Employ an implementation framework that lets you rollout the why and the what for the selected initiatives to every person in the organization. This framework must enable every team member to connect the dots between their job and the new initiatives. It must include accountability mechanisms and a scoring framework so that everyone knows how the organization is progressing toward its strategic initiatives.

If you want to safeguard the long-term health and viability of your organization, you need to do a regular strategic planning exercise. The discipline of critically evaluating your organization and making measured course corrections is the best insurance I know to keep you out of the trash heap of irrelevant, failed enterprises.

If you want more information on the strategic planning framework I use, contact me at mchirveno@clearvision.consulting.

WEEK 40 :: GOVERNANCE :: ORGANIZATIONAL STRUCTURE

There aren't very many things in the course of growing a business that a business owner "falls into," and there shouldn't be. Each move should be calculated and deliberate. But if there's one thing that happens, almost automatically, it's the organizational structure.

If an electrician starts a new business, the first hire is most likely another electrician. But as the business grows, there might be an accountant, then a customer service rep, then a procurement person, then an IT person...you get the idea. Each of these people become the de facto head of a department, and voila, you have a traditional Functional Organizational Structure.

Most of the small businesses I know have this structure, and most of the time it works well. And I'm guessing the boss spends very little spare thought time considering another option.

This week's One-Year, Thirty-Minute Business Transformation isn't an exhortation to change your organization's current structure but instead an encouragement to ponder the pluses and minuses inherent in that structure and to consider whether another structure might make it easier to execute your mission and push you closer to achieving your vision.

The functional organization structure is easy and intuitive. There are three primary advantages to the functional structure:

- **Focus.** The finance folks direct their attention to finance, the IT folks to IT, the production folks to production, etc. Unlike the solo practitioner who is salesperson, accountant, service provider, and janitor, people who work in a functional structure can train all their attention to a single discipline. This, theoretically, produces superior work, allows for narrow specialization, and lessens the probability for dropping the ball in that discipline.

- **Collaboration.** Having the software developers together or all the salespeople together allows them to bounce ideas off one another, work in tandem on projects, and encourages mentorship.

- **Redundancy.** Having multiple people working in the same discipline allows for cross training and for one person to have a working knowledge of the responsibilities of a coworker. This mitigates the risk of a "single point of failure." If one person gets hit by the proverbial bus, the work of the company goes on uninterrupted.

However, the functional structure has a couple of built-in challenges as well:

- **Handoffs.** Every organization I work with struggles with handoffs. How does the new customer order flow seamlessly from sales to production to accounting to customer service? How do we make sure that nothing falls through the cracks? How do we make sure the customer service rep has complete visibility into all the information they need to service the customer just as soon as the order is taken? As the boss, if you want your functional structure to work, focus your attention on handoffs.

- **Alignment.** As the organization grows, functional areas can sometimes take on a life of their own, especially if a particular discipline is preeminent in the value-creation activities of the company. A software company might elevate the importance of brilliant software developers, or a company in a very competitive commoditized industry might elevate the importance of a few star salespeople who can land large, lucrative clients and gain market share. These are good things. Excellent performers should be recognized. But the difficulties begin when some functional areas begin to wag the dog—when production becomes the enemy of the salespeople who procured the killer order that now must be fulfilled, or advertising becomes the enemy of editorial who claim that taking advertising from a particular business will compromise the journalistic integrity of the enterprise. As the boss, it's your job to keep every functional area on the same side of the equation.

- **Kingdom building.** A possible ugly symptom of failed alignment, a bad apple in the management ranks can begin to "kingdom build." Amassing an outsized staff or exercising undue influence in the organization is unhealthy. It's your responsibility to build an idea meritocracy where the best ideas rule the day, not the overgrown influence of a single person or department. Kingdom builders have ceased to look out for the good of the organization and are focused on their own enrichment.

I want to look at two other organizational structure options for small- and medium-sized enterprises.

The Matrix Structure has the components of a functional structure, but project or product teams cut laterally across the functions. The idea is to eliminate handoff problems by creating a multidiscipline team that focuses on a project or product with representatives who act as the authority and proxy for the discipline they represent.

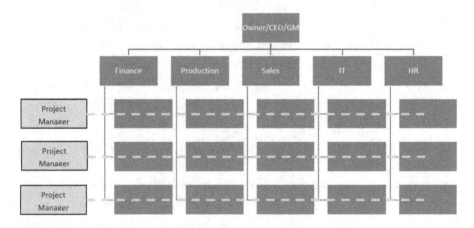

The first thing you probably noticed is the very thing that makes this structure challenging. People have two bosses—a straight line to a functional boss and a dotted line to a project or product manager. So to whom do they listen when priorities are conflicting? Typically, employees give more allegiance to the boss that has the greatest ability to make their life better (i.e., does their performance review, gives them raises, affects their upward mobility in the company, etc.). This structure can work, but the mechanics of the dual reporting must be crystal clear to the functional boss, the project manager, and the employee.

The Product Team Structure works to remove the dual reporting problem.

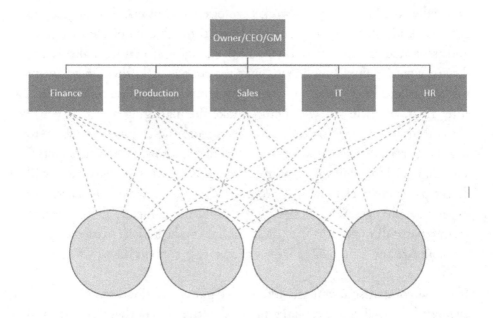

In this structure, the employee truly reports to the product or project manager but keeps a dotted line relationship back to the functional area they represent. This dotted line relationship attaches them to resources for collaboration with others in the same discipline and maybe even provides some redundancy for their work, but they are tied to the project/product team. The project manager is their boss (i.e., does their review, gives them raises, affects their upward mobility in the company, etc.). Representatives of each discipline (depending on the size and complexity of the project, there might be multiple people representing each discipline) are true cross-discipline collaborators since their fortunes are more strongly tied to the success of the project than they are to the functional area they represent.

I've laid these out a bit more cut and dried than they have to be. Certainly, companies can morph them to work for their particular situation. For example, in either the matrix or product team structures, functional and project bosses could collaborate on employee reviews instead of an either/or situation.

So finally, let's jump into this week's exercise. For this one, I'd suggest you get your leadership team together and step through each of the structures and associated pros and cons. If you think changing structures makes sense, discuss what it would look like to make the change. Ask why: Do you want to change because you're doing a subpar job managing in the current structure? If so, why will a new structure make the managing better? If you're convinced a new structure is desirable, explore the changes necessary to make the transition. How will the responsibilities of managers and supervisors change? How will the responsibilities of employees change? How will career paths change? How will processes change? How will the customer experience change? Will these changes build the company culture you're trying to install/maintain? Will these changes make it easier to execute your mission? Are any technology changes necessary to support the new structure?

If in the comparison, you feel like you've got the optimal structure now, evaluate how well you're capitalizing on the strengths of that structure and how well you're dealing with the weaknesses. Identify corrective action items for anything that you need to fix or exploit and assign them to someone. Get it on your calendar to check back in a couple of weeks to track progress.

Since you're a reader of the One-Year, Thirty-Minute Business Transformation, it's unlikely you're the CEO of a global enterprise. That was never the target audience. So the chances that you need an organizational structure that spans multiple business units or multiple large geographies are slim. But if you need to examine organizational structures that are more complex, check the resource page for this chapter on the oneyearthirtyminute.com website.

WEEK 41 :: LEADERSHIP :: HARD SKILLS AND SOFT SKILLS

Over the last couple of decades, we've collectively "seen the light" on Hard Skills vs. Soft Skills. To maximize our own effectiveness as a leader, we know we need both hard skills and soft skills. When we screen potential employees, we've added tools to assess not just hard skills—proficiency in a particular programming language, driving a forklift, tax planning, creating a PowerPoint deck, etc.—but also soft skills. We want to know if the potential team member is empathetic, a team player, a good communicator, a good problem solver, and more.

You and every employee in your organization come to the office, factory, hospital, or studio with a unique combination of personality, innate abilities, life experiences, and education that has shaped your current set of hard skills and soft skills. Those factors have an oversized influence on how easily you'll be able to continue honing those existing skills and adding new ones. Those with healthy self-awareness are a leg up on those who are blissfully ignorant of their own skills deficit. Those with good lateral thinking skills might have an advantage over those with only vertical thinking skills, depending on the new skill they are trying to master.

This week's One-Year, Thirty-Minute Business Transformation is an exercise in adding soft-skill and hard-skill components to your employee development program. If you don't have an employee development program, you need one, and you can find a framework on oneyearthirtyminute.com.

A good Employee Development Program aligns the interests of the employee with the interests of the company. Achieving growth goals benefits the organization and the individual. As goals are determined and milestones are set, a mix of hard-skill and soft-skill mastery punctuates the path.

Translating the learning of a hard skill to employee development exercises is straightforward:

- Read a manual

- Take a class (online or in-person)

- Become an apprentice

And proving mastery of the skill is equally objective:

- Take a test

- Demonstrate a technique

- Produce a product

- Speak the new language

You get the idea.

But I'm afraid mastering a new soft skill seems "squishier." It is, after all, a soft skill. So how can we integrate soft-skill development activities into our employee development program? HR sites are chock-full of lists of desirable soft skills. You'll find items like empathy, teamwork, communication, problem-solving, work ethic, creativity, adaptability, and many, many more. So during that employee development meeting, how are you going to get that team member to learn empathy, and how are they going to prove they did it?

Since none of us have a magic Geiger-counter that we can wave over a teammate and detect empathy, problem-solving, or any other soft skill, we have to translate that skill into actions we can use to teach the skill and to evaluate mastery of that skill. In employee development meetings, we need to connect the dots between the desired soft skill and the action, so the team member starts to think, "When I do this action, I'm giving outward evidence of this soft skill."

So here's this week's exercise. For your direct reports, make a list of the hard skills and soft skills you'd like them to add in the next twelve months; it shouldn't be more than one or two of each. For each of the skills, identify the how. For the hard skills, it might be take a class or work with another team member who has that skill and is able to act as a mentor (that mentor might be you). For the soft skills, translate them into observable, executable actions that the employee can begin to practice. To give you a head start, I'm giving you a few activities that translate into some of the most sought-after soft skills.

- **Listen when you'd normally offer an opinion.** This change in behavior can help build empathy, synthesis (creating a "mash-up" of previously uncombined ideas, methodologies or technologies), and problem-solving. Don't listen to respond better. Listen to understand more fully. Practice active listening activities like notetaking, repeating back the salient points of the speaker in your own words, and nodding your head when the speaker says something you agree with.

- **Ask good questions.** When you're tempted to start a conversation with a statement, use a question instead. Replace "Send out an email blast to all our existing customers announcing our new extended warranty" with "What do you think about using an email blast to announce our new extended warranty?" Use a methodology like the "Five Whys" to probe deeper if you feel like the current discussion is addressing a "branch" and not the "root" of an issue. Questions promote teamwork and collaboration, and the ensuing conversation provides an opportunity to practice the mentor mindset.

- **Look for the common ground first.** Team members with a more operational bent can sometimes easily find the ten problems a new initiative will create without acknowledging the upside of the initiative. They see the upside, but they quickly run to solve the problems first, so the initiative can work. On purpose, acknowledge the upside of new ideas before jumping into areas of disagreement or potential problems. If you can't get on board at all with the methodology, see if you can agree that your coworker has identified a problem worth solving: "I couldn't agree more that we have to solve this hold-time problem. Let's hammer away at this and see if we can figure out the best customer experience possible." This approach fosters collaboration and problem-solving.

- **Deliberately get out of your intellectual comfort zone.** Read a book or listen to a podcast authored by someone that doesn't share your political bent, professional expertise, or approach to life. For the content that espouses a different perspective, the opportunity to hold two differing opinions in your head at the same time (yours and the author's) encourages problem-solving (enumerating and evaluating the merits of two opposing views), empathy (learning why the author holds those views), and lateral thinking. For the content that explains a skill set different than yours, the ability to understand the degree of complexity in another discipline encourages teamwork (as you appreciate someone else's skill set) and synthesis.

- **Ask for a critique.** This might be the toughest one on the list. Ask two or three people (whom you respect and would go to for advice) to critique your communication style, management style, or leadership ability. Receiving the feedback graciously and openly displays adaptability and a commitment to lifelong learning.

- **Find a way to help a coworker succeed.** Look for a team member with a perpetually tough job or maybe one with a new, challenging assignment and figure out what you can do to help. Be a mentor, run interference so they can get the resources they need, or provide additional support from your department. Making an investment when you're not promised anything in return shows teamwork, mentor mindset, and empathy.

- **Look for a better way.** Find an existing activity in the organization and look for a way to make it better. Can you more effectively engage employees, communicate more clearly with customers, or take steps out of a process (and keep the quality intact or maybe even improve it)? Improving an activity demonstrates creativity, adaptability, and problem-solving.

- **Come in early and stay late and don't waste time during the workday.** This might seem like a no-brainer, but putting in a full day shows work ethic.

- **Ask for extra, more challenging work.** In addition to looking for a better way and putting in extra time, ask your boss for a challenging assignment or "the task nobody wants." Executing on this extra work shows adaptability, problem-solving, and a commitment to lifelong learning.

- **Learn how to write code.** It doesn't matter what your job is, if you want to learn to think in a linear way (vertically) and to never leave any stone unturned, learn a programming language. Software will only do what you tell it to do. If it's wrong, you get immediate feedback in the form of erroneous results. If it's incomplete, you have immediate feedback in the form of circumstances that aren't addressed. It's a shortcut to linear thinking, problem-solving, detail orientation, zooming out and zooming in, research, and creativity.

- **Learn how to draw.** In contrast to the previous bullet point, if you want to learn to think laterally, learn to zoom out and zoom in (for a whole different reason) and be creative—take an art class.

When you've finished this exercise for your direct reports, schedule a one-on-one meeting, discuss the growth in skills you'd like to see, and agree on the specific action items, timeline, check-in schedule, and metrics for measuring progress. Encourage your direct reports to do the same thing with their team members.

WEEK 42 :: MARKETING :: FIVE FORCES PLUS ONE

When vending your products and services, you spend a lot of time pressing out:

- You create new products and services you believe current and potential customers will want.

- You tweak existing products and services to keep them attractive to current and potential customers.

- You improve the customer experience to encourage loyalty and decrease defection.

- You create new messaging to tell your story in a more compelling way.

But any healthy assessment of an organization's competitive environment asks the question, "What is pressing back against us?" Competitors, customers, vendors, and the environment at large are always changing. So in addition to the proactive "pressing out," you must counterpunch—not necessarily responding tit for tat but tracking what's going on around you and responding when advantageous.

Michael Porter introduced his "Five Forces Model" in 1979. Forty years later, it's still an effective way to examine the competitive forces in your industry.

In the mid-1990s, a sixth force was added to the model (some folks have credited it to Andy Grove, the former Intel CEO).

In this week's One-Year, Thirty-Minute Business Transformation, we're going to walk through the six forces and ask questions that will help you look critically at what is "pressing back" at you. Then, more importantly, we'll suggest some "counterpunching" options you can evaluate with your team.

Rivalry among existing competitors. Other companies serving the same customers and/or offering products similar to yours, pose, in some ways, the stickiest problem. The gut reaction to lower prices only sets up a race to the bottom as each competitor settles for less and less revenue to pick up a few more points of market share. Competing on price is an unsustainable tactic. So for products that are largely undifferentiated, what can you do instead? The short answer is to change the basis of competition. Overnight package delivery is big business, but since the end result is a package moved from point A to point B overnight, it's highly undifferentiated. The competitors in this industry have done a good job of turning our attention to unique competencies that distinguish them from their competitors, package tracking and outsourced logistics providers to name a couple. So if you find yourself in a slugfest with a capable competitor, consider this:

- Are the products or services truly undifferentiated, or have you done a substandard job explaining your unique value proposition?

- If they are truly indistinguishable (electrical outlet covers, for instance), can you shift the basis of competition to a unique delivery competency or customer experience?

- Can you move up or down to premium or economy versions of the product and capture an "end" of the market?

- Can you leverage the competencies that allow you to create this product and use them in a "blue ocean"—one that's free from the bloody red waters of your war with current competitors?

Threat of New Entrants. If you're making money, someone else would love to make it as well. Any successful enterprise is going to draw the attention of existing companies looking for new opportunities and startups looking to crash a successful party. There's an important discipline that comes into play here that we discussed in an earlier One-Year, Thirty-Minute Business Transformation—Creative Destruction. Creative destruction is the practice of scrutinizing your current products and processes to make sure they are impervious to competitors and, if they are not, replacing them so that they are. If you're not engaging in this exercise, potential new entrants will be. So how do we stave off new entrants?

- Build a great database and communicate with the people in it frequently. In theory, you know infinitely more about your market than a new entrant does. Use your experience to be a better listener, understanding the needs of the market more accurately than potential new entrants. Tell your story in a meaningful way.

- Give great service. Don't give customers a reason to look elsewhere for the same good or service.

- Leverage the learning curve that you've already ascended. That learning curve should translate into better vendor relationships, more mature processes, and, consequently, lower costs. You should be able to price match or even undercut a new entrant and still make more money because your costs are lower.

- One last, more radical idea. If a new competitor is exceedingly capable, maybe you should buy them. Unless they are incredibly well capitalized, they might have shot the wad creating their new product or service.

Threat of Substitute Products. This force is different from competition with existing rivals because it considers enterprises competing for the same dollars, such as going to the movie theater vs. streaming a movie at home or playing mini golf vs. going to the movie theater. Substitute products can span industry types—gym membership (a service) vs. buying a Peloton bike (a product with an optional subscription service). Value creation is always a holy grail exercise, but, in this case, it's really the entire discussion. How can you create an offering of surpassing value for this particular dollar?

- What is the desired end result for this expenditure? Get healthy, be entertained, not be hungry anymore, or be confident that my car is safe and reliable again?

- What stands in the way of the customer achieving that goal? How can you most efficiently and convincingly eradicate those obstacles?

- What pushes them closer to that goal? How can you most efficiently and convincingly show them that your solution takes them faster and farther toward that goal?

- How can you communicate that you "get it" and that your methodology for reaching their goal affords them complete control, provides the biggest bang for the buck, overcomes all of their objections, and checks every box (or at least checks the boxes better than all available alternatives)?

Bargaining Power of Customers. You know intuitively that customers have power, but in some circumstances their power is outsized. If a customer's defection leaves you with a ton of unrecovered acquisition costs (i.e., it cost you a bunch of money to get the customer to buy the first time, and they've not made enough purchases to offset those costs) or, on the other end of the spectrum, if one or two customers represent such a large part of your revenue that their departure could cripple or destroy your company, those customers exercise substantial control over your company.

- It seems a counterintuitive, but how can you inflict some pain on the customer if they leave? I don't mean real pain, of course, but something like loyalty points or a discount that can only be redeemed on a future purchase. Withhold that benefit until they transact more business.

- If your product or service is a bit more sophisticated, can you introduce some switching costs into the equation? If you provide a service like accounting or tax preparation, institute an onboarding regimen that involves a thorough (but valuable) data-gathering exercise where you not only gather historical financial data but discuss future financial goals. The prospect of spending that time again, with a new provider, might dissuade them from defecting.

- If one customer represents a significant percentage of your revenue ("high customer concentration" in finance lingo), there are a couple of things you might want to consider. If you service only one industry, can you solicit other potential clients in that industry and leverage your deep industry expertise? If servicing competitors poses a problem for your large client, change geography so that prospective client bases don't overlap. Or look for ways to leverage the skills you are using to service that client and find other industries where those skills are in demand. Project management, software development, process improvement, and a host of other skills are highly transferrable.

Bargaining Power of Suppliers. The risk with a powerful supplier is three-fold. They can drive up your costs with price increases because the materials they supply are unique or scarce. They can halt or cripple your value-creation activities by being late or erratic in delivery. Or they can negatively affect your quality by providing products that perform inconsistently.

- How can you create a partnership with a powerful supplier? How can you configure your relationship so that successes and failures are shared? For example, a retroactive per piece payment or bonus payment if every shipment in the previous quarter was on time and the defect rate was below 1 percent? Or penalty payments, like a .5 percent reduction in unit cost for each hour the production line was out of service because of a stockout on the part the vendor supplies?

- How can you give them greater visibility into your processes, so they can see how their product is utilized and when it will be reordered next (so they can prepare for production)?

- How can you leverage their expertise to improve quality and drive down costs as you contemplate future versions of their product? How early can you bring them into the discussion? If you help them build ease of manufacturing into future versions, costs can come down.

Complementary Products. We are awash in manifestations of this competitive force—razors and blades, phones and cases, phones and apps, printers and ink, etc. But leveraging this for competitive advantage has some fairly straightforward components.

- Can you clearly see the beginning and ending of the complementary wave you're riding? If you make cell phone cases, you'll be retooling every eight to twelve months. If you make ink cartridges for printers, a model could be in use for several years. Complementary products also vary in complexity: a VHS tape had moving parts, but a DVD had none.

- Will you be directly benefitting from both sides of the equation? Will you be making razors and blades, or will you only be making blades?

- If the complementary products are in the tech realm, is the successor technology likely to be in your wheelhouse? Streaming video is not at all like Blu-ray players and Blu-ray discs. Can you be proficient in, and can you afford to play in, very disparate spaces?

In almost every case, the things you do to press out will be more important than the things that are pressing in, but you can't ignore the environment in which you complete.

WEEK 43 :: FINANCE :: OPERATING BUDGET

According to a survey by Clutch, 61 percent of small-business owners did not create an annual operating budget. As the number of employees decreased, the likelihood of a business creating an annual budget fell even more—74 percent of businesses with one to ten employees did not create a budget. Unsurprisingly, in another Clutch survey, 35 percent of small-business owners listed unforeseen expenses as their top financial challenge.

An Operating Budget certainly doesn't insulate you from unforeseen expenses, but it does force you to deliberately examine projected revenue and expense numbers for the upcoming financial period. The exercise, if done correctly, will make you prove, with real math, that your strategic and operational plans are going to deliver the financial results you desire.

Earlier in the One-Year, Thirty-Minute Business Transformation we looked at capital budgeting. Operating budgets differ radically from capital budgets. Capital budgets deal with large-ticket items that are depreciated over several years. Their purchase is not reflected in an operating budget. Operating budgets deal with income and expense projections for an upcoming fiscal period, money that is typically both earned and spent in that period.

Operating budgets are based on assumptions: For example *What we pay for utilities will stay the same. We will have no major customer defections. Our health care premiums will go up 10 percent.* At the beginning of the budgeting period, you've got to validate every assumption as much as possible. It's also prudent to document assumptions so everyone involved knows the "facts" the budget was built on.

Clearly your thirty-minute exercise this week isn't long enough to pull together a budget, so the goal is to pull together a budget plan, get the plan to the right people, and be able to clearly explain your budget methodology.

According to the Corporate Finance Institute, there are four methods for putting together an operating budget:

- **Incremental.** Start with last year's actual revenue and expense numbers and ratchet them up or down based on a percentage or on anticipated changes in specific budget categories. I'm not a fan of this methodology, since it's easy to perpetuate a budget that might have been built incorrectly in the beginning. And it might be feeding budget categories that are no longer relevant to the success of the business.

- **Activity-based.** This method begins with revenue targets, then fleshes out the expenses needed to reach those revenue targets. This methodology works well for "cost of goods sold" expenses but might be a bit unruly when building the underlying administrative costs.

- **Value proposition.** This approach requires every expense to be tied back to some value-creation activity for the customer, employee, shareholder, or other stakeholder. I like the premise here because, truly, if an activity doesn't bring value, then why do it?

- **Zero-based.** Every single budget line begins at zero. From scratch, you must build every line item. Consequently, the existence of the line item and the amount must be justified. I like this one also because of the discipline required and the scrutiny given to each entry.

You can choose one of these methodologies or a hybrid of two or three. The methodology takes a backseat to the real reason for doing a budget—*to correctly fund value-creation activities so that projected revenue goals are met or exceeded, and expenses are right-sized so that all stakeholders receive returns that cement their relationship to the company.* This incredibly important point deserves a bit more attention. Customer-facing activities must be sufficiently funded so that purchasers receive a product or service that exceeds their expectations and is delivered in a way that makes them feel good about their purchase. Employee compensation must keep value producers inside the organization happy and engaged and not looking for employment elsewhere. Shareholders must receive a sufficient return, so their investment in the organization continues to be justified. A similar calculation must be made for every stakeholder in the organization.

Let's jump into a few mechanics for budget building.

- **Involve the people ultimately accountable for hitting the numbers.** The directors and managers who will reap the rewards or bear the consequences for financial performance for the budget entity (department, division, or business unit) must create the budget for that entity. If they're smart, they'll involve other team members who will impact that entity's performance.

- **Simultaneously work bottom up and top down.** Expectations for profitability should be communicated down and needs for funding value-creation activities should be communicated up. The organization's desired endgame should be baked into the company culture and should be a regularly discussed topic in the organization, so there shouldn't be any surprises here. This is just an annual exercise dedicated to examining the financial manifestations of what you're after every day.

- **Use tools that make sense.** A smaller organization might get away with an Excel template used by everyone in the organization. Larger organizations probably want to opt for some of the more robust budgeting tools available.

- **Use the right level of detail.** In your office supply category, you don't need a line item for pencils, another for staples, and another for paper clips. If you do, you have the wrong people in charge. Budgets reflect the level of autonomy in that business entity.

- **Budgets should include contingencies, but those building the budgets should know that the ultimate determinant of investment is value creation.** I'm in favor of adding some contingencies to a budget (for unforeseen circumstances like overtime, equipment failure, and the opportunity to capture an emergent opportunity), but ultimately every expenditure in an organization should be about value creation. If a situation arises that affords an opportunity for value creation, even though that opportunity was not apparent at budget creation time, the person responsible for that budget entity should know that they can come to you with that opportunity and not be chastised for considering something "not in the budget."

- **Budgets function as a "reality check" for projected revenue and projected expense.** Let's say your budgeted revenue reflects the sale of 3 million widgets. What is the sales commission for 3 million widgets? What is the cost of raw materials for 3 million widgets? What is the labor cost for 3 million widgets, the answer of which requires you to know how long it takes to make each individual widget? Will any overtime be required to produce 3 million widgets? Is the present capacity of your plant sufficient to produce 3 million widgets? What does it cost to ship 3 million widgets? Will the production of 3 million widgets force you to add another shift? What will be the cost of supervisors for that shift? Are all those items in your budget? The budgeting process is the mechanism that ensures you've accurately identified and synced all of the revenue and costs associated with the value-creation activities that get you to your financial targets.

- **At some point in the process, check your work against industry benchmarks.** I'm not a big "best practices" person. Every "best practice" was once a wild idea gambled on by some innovative thinker. I'd prefer to put my money on the innovative thinker. That being said, it's not a bad idea to check your work against your competitors just to make sure you're not missing something. For instance, you can easily find stats on what percent of revenue is spent on Information Technology in your industry. If your competitors are spending 4 percent of revenue on IT, and you're spending 2 percent, maybe you're not being thrifty. Maybe you're missing opportunities to automate work or offer new tech-enabled products.

- **Bake in profit margins at the budget level.** If you want to make a profit of 20 percent, make sure your revenue and expense projections enforce that margin. Engineer the value-creation activities until you've pushed the revenue and expense numbers far enough apart to hit your profit target.

Get the responsible parties together and lay out your plan. If this is your first budget, it's important to explain your rationale. It's all about the discipline—the same reason you do a strategic plan or any other deliberate planning activity. It's the opportunity to step away from the press of all the things that clamor for your attention and focus on, in this case, the finances of your organization.

After your budget is in place, check your performance against it regularly. Make it a part of your balanced scorecard. When opportunities come to deviate from it, use it as a development opportunity for your staff as you discuss the rationale behind decisions to "stick to it" or "stray from it."

WEEK 44 :: STRATEGIC PLANNING :: ABSORPTIVE CAPACITY

One of the most disconcerting things any business leader contends with is "disequilibrium." Disequilibrium is that queasy feeling when what you think you know for sure is, all of a sudden, in question. One moment, your world is tidy—all the pieces make sense—and now, suddenly, it doesn't. Disequilibrium happens in all parts of life, not just work: faith, relationships, health, and the list goes on. But for this week's One-Year, Thirty-Minute Business Transformation, we'll discuss work.

Sales are humming along. Everyone loves your product. You have to beat customers off with a stick. Then, a little-known competitor introduces a product that upends your industry. Customers flock to your competitor, and your revenue plummets. Yesterday, revenue projections for the next couple of quarters looked stellar. Today, with the money on hand, you'll only be able to make payroll for eight more weeks.

Now what? Disequilibrium, that situation when new information comes into your world and throws everything you know out of sync, reveals your Absorptive Capacity. Absorptive capacity is the ability to synthesize the new information you've received, reconcile it to what you knew before, and respond in a way that reflects your new understanding, all while pushing toward your vision and fulfilling your mission.

Before jumping into this week's exercise, let's illustrate with an incredibly oversimplified example. You sell cameras and the film that goes inside those cameras. People point the camera at an image, push a button, and the image is etched on the film. After those people have taken a few dozen of those pictures, they send the film to a third party that puts the film through a process and prints the images from the film on special paper. That's how pictures are made. Everyone knows that. Then, one day, you learn of a new camera. People point that camera at an image, push a button, and the image is translated into millions of electronic picture elements (pixels) organized on a grid and saved on a silicon chip. No film. No third party. No printing on paper. The little chip holds hundreds of images, and the images are completely portable and can be sent to other people using a variety of electronic devices. You've just experienced disequilibrium. What you thought you knew about taking pictures has been disrupted with new, confusing information.

What you do next determines what your business will look like going forward. You can deny the new information: *The way we do pictures is what customers will want forever. This is a passing fad. This will never be commercially viable.* Or you can demonstrate your absorptive capacity by synthesizing the new information and begin making positive progress toward your vision armed with an updated understanding of the environment in which you compete.

Let's jump into this week's exercise. It's not possible to engineer a moment of disequilibrium. That's part of the reason they're so jarring. They come out of the blue. So for this week's exercise, we want to create a framework that you can use to lead yourself and your team through these events when they come. In that framework, we want to strengthen your organization's absorptive capacity, so you emerge from disequilibrium stronger and more prepared to reach your vision.

Understand exactly what's threatened by the new information. Is your entire business model in jeopardy like the camera illustration above? Is your workforce in danger of being poached (a large employer with deep pockets is building a new plant in your city and will be hiring thousands)? Are your customer's expectations likely to radically change (there's a better product available or better pricing for a competing product)? What problem is being solved now more effectively than you were solving it before? This is no time to "whistle while you walk through the graveyard." Instead, it's time for radical truth telling. Get your most trusted team members together and ask hard questions. Talk to current and existing customers to gauge their response to the new information; depending on the information, it might or might not affect them. Define the breadth and depth of the impact from the new information.

Identify the downstream effects. What's the impact on revenue? Does existing equipment become obsolete? Do existing core competencies become meaningless? Does customer acquisition messaging need to be reworked? Is your cost of goods sold or customer pricing impacted?

Envision the new reality. No one has a crystal ball, but using your best judgment, envision the new world created with the new information. Who will win? Who will lose? What will the winners have done to win? What will the losers have done (or not done) to lose? What vendor resources will become important? What will be important to employees? What will be important to customers? What will be important to other stakeholders—shareholders, regulators, vendors?

Create alternatives. With your new, expanded understanding, create multiple scenarios that make sense in the new reality. For each scenario, push toward effective value creation and push toward fulfilling your vision. Can new, capable competitors become strategic partners? Can new, capable competitors become acquisition targets? Should you become an acquisition target for a new, capable competitor? Can you successfully emulate a new product or service offering? Can you move up or down in the value-creation chain? Is there talent you need to acquire now? Are there assets you need to jettison now? What becomes the new, valuable core competency?

Leverage existing knowledge and experience. When faced with a challenge, your gut reaction is to do what you already do except do it faster, with more intensity, and with higher quality. I get it. But if you're riding a bicycle, you'll never go faster or farther or carry more than your new, capable competitor who's driving a delivery van. That's where your knowledge and experience become your competitive advantage. You know the limits of your current team, know your current model, and know the needs and wants of your customer base.

Leverage existing relationships. Tap the collective genius of employees, vendors, and even customers. If you don't have one already, establish a true idea meritocracy, an environment where the best idea wins the day no matter whose idea it is. Beware of the HIPPO (the Highest-Paid Person's Opinion).

Look for meaning in adjacent areas. Does the new information or the new reality it produces allow you to pivot to an adjacent area? Many years ago, during a downturn in general aviation sales, manufacturers of small planes become subcontractors for commercial airline manufacturers (whose business was booming) building wings, tail sections, and other subassemblies for them. Can you leverage existing capabilities into new opportunities?

Look for meaning in other industries. Are there other industries that were faced with a similar situation? How did the players in those industries respond? How did the actions of the winners differ from the actions of the losers?

Fire bullets. When you're ready to test your responses, as much as possible, fire bullets: small, controlled, cheap tests to evaluate the promise of that response. Tweak and test again until you have an effective response to the new reality. You can read about firing bullets in an earlier One-Year, Thirty-Minute Business Transformation.

Measure and adjust. As you roll out your new response, measure the factors that accurately indicate that you've successfully reacted to the new environment. Depending on your unique situation, these might include measurements like no decrease in customer retention, no loss of revenue, no increase in cost of goods sold, and/or stable customer satisfaction scores. Whatever the metric, continue to evolve your response as the metrics dictate.

The speed of change in the competitive environment continues to accelerate. And the magnitude of the changes continues to increase. Increasing your absorptive capacity is a critical skill to ensure that your business continues to not only stay relevant but also prospers in an increasingly turbulent business environment.

WEEK 45 :: GOVERNANCE :: ON THE BUSINESS VS. IN THE BUSINESS

Working on the business instead of in the business. I'm not sure Michael Gerber was the first one to introduce the phrase, but I'm pretty sure no one was more responsible for making it a permanent part of our business lexicon than Gerber in his 1986 book, *The E Myth.* He told us something we all know deep down: entrepreneurs aren't superheroes. They're not imbued with special powers that let them build a business from scratch and become successful and wealthy while the rest of us work for someone else. He did however teach us that those entrepreneurs who reach the tipping point and build a real business (as opposed to those who just created a job for themselves) learned how to work *on* their business and not just *in* it.

Working *in* the business is that natural tendency to gravitate towards operational activities that generate revenue—making a sandwich and delivering it to a patron's table, unclogging a toilet, or writing a contract. Clearly, if these activities ceased, the company would go out of business, so they can't be neglected. But those entrepreneurs who created enduring enterprises learned to work *on* the business. They trained and empowered others to do much of the important transactional work while they focused on making the business itself healthier—building a strong team with a vibrant culture, creating bulletproof processes that guarantee consistent product delivery, consistently filling the sales pipeline, being financially disciplined, and more.

However, gravitating toward working *in* the business isn't just the affliction of novice entrepreneurs who haven't made the leap. All of us can fall prey to the tyranny of daily, transactional work that isn't in the best long-term interest of the organization. So, in this week's One-Year, Thirty-Minute Business Transformation, we want to create a framework that you and your team can use to keep your focus on long-term organizational health and do it in a way that fits each person's responsibilities in the organization.

There's no "right" percentage of your work week you should be devoting to working *on* the business instead of *in* it. But the farther you are up the food chain, the higher the percentage should be. If you're the big boss, the overwhelming majority of your work should be devoted to organizational health, staff development, and business growth. For those farther down the food chain, the mix can and should change to allow for more operational responsibilities (working *in* the business).

Let's jump in. I want you to do a couple of things during your thirty-minute exercise this week—identify the best on-the-business activities you can prioritize during your week and add some tools to your toolbox that will help you protect your on-the-business time.

I can't tell you all the activities that best constitute working *on* the business for you and your organization, but I want to give you a starter list. Jot the ones that resonate with you into Evernote or on a notepad. At the end of the exercise, we're going to use them.

- **Spend time on personal growth.** Read a book, listen to a podcast, take a class, go to a conference. Your organization will most likely never grow beyond you. Learn from people who don't agree with you philosophically, who work in other industries, and who have already walked this road before you. Synthesize the new things you learn: How do they fit with what you know already? How do they conflict with what you know already? How should what you have learned impact the organization?

- **Devote time to staff development.** How can you prepare your direct reports for more responsibilities, including assuming your job? What parts of their performance are deficient? Do they have sufficient cross-discipline understanding? How well are they developing their team so that their eventual replacement is ready? Are they creating sufficient margin in their operational responsibilities, so they have time to devote to working *on* the business? Is there talent missing in the organization?

- **Examine meaningful metrics.** Have you identified the metrics that are truly indicative of organizational health? If so, are you tracking them faithfully and making course corrections based on the data? Are you pushing them down through the organization so that everyone knows whether or not the organization is "winning"?

- **Evaluate your value-creation activities.** Are you solving your customer's problems more effectively than others in your industry? If not, why not? What changes can you make to your value-creation activities so that you are creating value better than your competitors? Can you improve delivery of your product or service so that customers are less likely to defect?

- **Survey the industry landscape.** Are there new, capable competitors in the industry? How does their offering or delivery differ from yours? Where are your products in the product life cycle? Are any successor products on the horizon? If so, what is the right response right now? Are there any regulatory changes that could alter the dynamic in your industry? Are there any shifts in the macroenvironment that that could impact your industry or business—financial (cost of money, availability of credit), technological, cultural norms, or environmental norms?

- **Spend time with several stakeholder groups.** Get out of the office for meaningful dialogue with team members, customers, vendors, shareholders, and more. Ask good questions. Probe for understanding when it comes to things that are hindering them in value-creation activities. Synthesize all the information you receive to get to the truth. Recognize that the information you receive from each stakeholder group is colored by their experience and interests. Remember, we don't see things as they are; we see them as we are.

- **Guard the culture.** Nothing is more important than modeling the culture and communicating the culture. Every stakeholder group needs to see you exhibit and explain the "____ Company Way" to treat each other, customers, vendors, and shareholders and how to approach work.

If those are ways to work *on* the business, what do you do when the daily press of work tries to drag you back to working *in* the business? These tools will help.

- **Reframe the task.** When an urgent operational problem lands on your desk, identify the process that failed (a flaw in the order process, an untrained employee, tech that failed, a vendor that didn't deliver, etc.) and fix both the immediate problem and the root cause. If you trace back every time, you're stopping the problem from happening again by improving organizational health.

- **Say no.** Some urgent matters don't deserve your attention. Someone else can worry about the malfunctioning garage door in the warehouse. Ego would like you to jump up from your desk and save the day, but working on the business requires you to say, "Have Mary in the warehouse call the company we used last time. And next time we have a problem with garage doors, you can go straight to Mary. She can take care of it."

- **Put employees first.** Every urgent problem screams to be solved now. It's almost always faster for you to solve the problem yourself. Resist the temptation. Instead, use it as a training opportunity. Grab the one, two, or six people that could solve this problem if they knew what you knew and walk them through the resolution, patiently answering every question. The next time this surfaces, hand it off to one of them and go back to working *on* the business.

- **Go from the outside in.** Keep problem-solving customer centric. Challenge team members to, instead of consulting you, do what's best for the customer. They can only interrupt you if they're unsure of what that is.

- **Be accountable.** None of us are immune from being pulled under by the current of urgent problems. Consequently, we need to give others in the organization permission to call us out when we're spending too much time working *in* the business instead of *on* it.

Lots of time management techniques fail miserably because they're built around open slots on a calendar. Here's an observation: I always have enough in-the-business tasks to fill my entire week. Take the tasks from the on-the-business list and put them on the calendar. Then, let nothing displace them. If the building is on fire, put it out, then return to your on-the-business task for that day and finish it. If something has to push, let it be one of the in-the-business tasks. Don't worry, it will be there tomorrow.

If you want a healthy organization with engaged employees and increasing revenue, this is the only way. You can never work *in* the business enough to make it happen.

WEEK 46 :: CULTURE :: CONFRONT THE BRUTAL FACTS

In 1546, English author John Heywood wrote, "There are none so blind as those who will not see." The formative years of my working life were spent in a declining industry. The descent was steep, but it became a lot steeper because people leading the organization failed to confront the brutal facts—in our particular case, the commercial use of the internet. As revenues declined, there was a lot of "whistling through the graveyard." Revenue was going directly to online competitors. Our "creative destruction" in response to the new online world looked more like repainting the bathroom instead of tearing down the house. In the late 1990s, I wrote a capital request for the purchase of a new management information system. The proposal included adding capabilities that leveraged our address-specific data with address-specific data from area utilities and presenting them together in an online portal. I proposed selling address-specific online billing services (we would have been the first) and selling the data to companies with an interest in address-specific information, such as realtors and home services. I was told to take that section out of my capital request because we didn't need it.

In my opening quote, Heywood wasn't disparaging those who couldn't see, but those who wouldn't see.

In his 2011 book *Good to Great*, Jim Collins encouraged business leaders to confront the brutal facts. Since I began consulting in 2006, it's been my unfortunate discovery that running from the truth is a common practice in many organizations. We know we should fire that disruptive employee. We know we should find a new vendor to replace that underperforming one. We know we should abandon that underperforming product or location. But we have an emotional attachment where those areas are concerned, so we don't act.

In week twenty-six of the One-Year, Thirty-Minute Business Transformation, I listed my Cultural Imperatives. Confronting the brutal facts is one of them. Just like Mentor Mindset in week four and Learning Orientation in week sixteen, Confronting the Brutal Facts deserves its own One-Year, Thirty-Minute Business Transformation.

So how do you create an organization that actively pursues the truth and has the organizational fortitude to act on it? In this week's exercise, I want you to critique your organization. I want you to look for truth-hiding behavior, check for practices that proactively unearth unpleasant truths, root out people not committed to radical transparency, and create or strengthen organizational backbone that acts based on the true picture the facts paint.

Let's jump in.

Truth-Hiding Behaviors

- You've rebuffed a peer or subordinate telling them, "Don't bring me problems, only bring me solutions." Maybe they don't have a solution, and since they don't, they fail to pass along information that is vital to the future of your organization.

- You spot a new competitor but discount them because you think the management of the company is weak or the initial product or service is subpar. Managers can grow, and products can evolve. Better to take the threat seriously and ask, "Why did they think there was room in my space for a new entrant? What is deficient in my product or delivery that makes them think there is opportunity?"

- You get negative feedback from an unreliable source (e.g., a less-than-stellar employee, an always-complaining customer, or a new, unproven vendor). Go ahead and explore their feedback. As my former boss used to say, "Even a wild boar finds a hickory nut every now and then."

- A problem keeps surfacing, and a peer or subordinate suggests that you're the cause of the problem (because of your management style, time management, lack of planning, etc.) You've discounted that feedback because you've successfully run the business for a number of years.

Unearthing Unpleasant Truths

- Make sure bad news can easily travel up and down in your organization. Make sure there are no reprisals for "truth tellers." As a matter of fact, recognize their efforts in getting all the facts on the table.

- Proactively ask for feedback from employees, customers, and suppliers. Make phone calls and send surveys. Take the totality of the feedback to create a balanced, accurate picture of what it's like to work at your company, purchase products or services from your company, or sell to your company.

- Engage the services of a third party who can bring a fresh perspective. Maybe a consultant, an advisory board, or business-owner peer from a networking group.

- Trust the data over your gut. Twenty years of experience can make you think you're invincible. Twenty years of connection can also make you emotionally tied to a person, place, or thing that needs to go.

Root Out People Not Committed to Radical Transparency

- Commit first and foremost to the purpose of the organization. Our natural inclination is to want to be right. Instead of putting a premium on being right, lead your organization to put a premium on the pursuit of truth.

- Embrace humility. As Ryan Holiday noted in *Ego is the Enemy*, "If your reputation can't absorb a few blows, it wasn't worth anything in the first place."

- Engage in vigorous discussions. Build trust inside your team so that you can talk to each other about failures in execution, faulty plans, and blown opportunities. The momentary discomfort of discussing individual lapses must be subordinate to the importance of resolving nagging problems or the exploiting of looming opportunities. If a team member can't exist in this environment, seriously consider their future in the organization.

- Squash every form of defensive behavior. When you hear things you'd rather not hear about your organization, your product, or your people, resist the temptation to defend. Instead, figure out what you can learn from the feedback and teach your team to do the same.

Strengthen Your Organizational Backbone

- Adopt an execution framework that will help you implement your fact-driven initiatives. There are several good ones available. I like Objectives and Key Results (OKR), Four Disciplines of Execution (4DX), Entrepreneur Operating System (EOS), and I have my own, The Business Framework.

- Don't let problems linger. Pursue continuous improvement. Create a bias for action.

- Build accountability inside the organization. Hold others accountable and have others hold you accountable.

When you finish your critique, pull your team together for a heartfelt chat. If you've failed to confront the brutal facts in the past, apologize and commit to do it in the future. Prioritize radical transparency, organizational truth telling, and fact-based decision-making. Act courageously based on the truth.

WEEK 47 :: MARKETING :: TARGET CLIENTS

Traditional marketing many times mimicked traditional product development. In traditional product development, a team of "experts" created a solution that they (1) were enamored with, (2) thought represented a departure from current products in function, usability, and/or experience, and (3) hoped had commercial viability. Companies then turned those products over to traditional marketers who touted the features and benefits of the new offerings in hopes that someone would be willing to part with their hard-earned money and give it a try. In short, a solution in search of a problem. Once those few, brave early adopters surfaced, the marketers could look for others like them—Target Clients.

For decades, the bulk of "marketing science" was built around this approach. We learned about market segmentation, customer profiles, demographics, psychographics, geographics, behavioristics, and a host of other ways to segregate and talk to people who might be interested in our products or services. I'm not advocating that we abandon or unlearn all or any of this; instead, we should broaden our field of knowledge. More recent research in product development and marketing is equipping us with information that can make us much more effective in creating new offerings and communicating with those who are willing to buy them.

In *Competing Against Luck*, Clayton Christensen helped us understand that the key to innovative product development is problem-solving. Yogi Berra reminded us that "you can observe a lot by watching." Together these two pieces of information give you everything you need to know to create a successful product. Carefully survey your slice of the world for a problem to solve. Then, solve the problem better than anyone else.

Problems and the subsequent solutions can be simple: your smartphone slides across the dashboard or seat when you're driving, so you need a bracket that fits in your cupholder with a slot on the top to hold your phone. Or the problems can be more obscure, so obscure that you didn't know you had the problem. Steve Jobs and the folks at Apple discovered that you needed a device bigger than your smartphone but smaller than your laptop, and voila, the iPad was born (along with a host of Android competitors). You didn't know you needed a tablet, but so far, about 1.5 billion of them have been sold worldwide. The potential upside of a product is in direct proportion to number of people that are afflicted by the problem that the product solves.

That brings us to this week's One-Year, Thirty-Minute Business Transformation.

For this week's exercise, I want you to create a detailed definition of the problem you're effectively solving—What is the cause? How does it manifest itself (i.e., what are the first-, second-, and third-order consequences? What is the personal impact? What is the financial impact? What is the emotional or psychological impact? What is the social impact?) Identify the people who have that problem. Those people are your target clients.

As you start the exercise, the most disturbing discovery could be that you've created a solution for a nonexistent problem or a problem that afflicts so few people it's not commercially viable. If that's the case, it's time to survey the landscape and look for a problem to solve.

Assuming you have a superior solution to a real problem experienced by enough people, the assignment becomes figuring out how to effectively communicate with the people afflicted by that problem. I want to offer up some bullet points:

- Discover where the people who have that problem look for information to solve it—Google search, friends on social media, LinkedIn, from others in their industry, cold sales calls, email solicitation, Yelp, Angie's List, networking groups, etc.

- Using their preferred medium, begin interacting with them by sharing information that convinces them you understand the depth of the problem. Discuss multiple manifestations of the problem and the impacts of the problem.

- Empathize with them. To prove the depth of your understanding, discuss the way the problem makes them feel—frustrated, insecure, uncertain about the future, etc.

- Start being useful. Offer initial solutions to the problem. If you give away valuable information, you show your care for your target clients and your commitment to solving their problem. And you build credibility as a trusted resource.

- Explain your value proposition—you have a good, workable solution that makes sense economically. You can't charge them ten dollars to solve a one-dollar problem.

- Let existing clients build your credibility. Show that you've successfully solved the problem for others by sharing testimonials, case studies, and white papers.

- Reach out to individual target clients with personalized emails (or for business-to-business, LinkedIn messages). Invite them into one-on-one conversations where you can probe for information on how the problem you solve impacts them.

As you explain your intimate understanding of the problem, your understanding of those afflicted by the problem, the pain they feel as a result, the epiphany that brought you to your solution to the problem, the thoroughness of the solution, the economic value of the solution, and the passion you bring to delivering the solution, you will gain recognition among those with the problem and will be seen as a valuable resource. You will find those who, as Simon Sinek would say, "share your why," or, as Seth Godin would say, "belong to your tribe."

In every interaction, probe for additional opportunities to listen and deepen your understanding of the problem and how it impacts potential target clients. And, in every interaction, if the target client is ready to buy, make your products or services available with an easy-to-follow call to action.

During this week's thirty-minute exercise, gather your team together. After you've defined the problem in sufficient detail, make your initial pass through the list above. Make notes. Decide on your initial medium and messaging.

As you get started, resist the temptation to be perfect. Just start. Experiment with messaging and medium. Every time you get a response, increase your understanding of the problem and how it affects your target clients. Soon you'll be effectively communicating with the people you've built your business to help.

WEEK 48 :: STRATEGIC PLANNING :: ALLIANCES

"If you want to go fast, go alone. If you want to go far, go together." This African proverb is the perfect backdrop for this week's One-Year, Thirty-Minute Business Transformation. If you're a solopreneur or the owner or CEO of a small company, you can pivot quickly. You don't need anyone's permission for a change in product, service, delivery, messaging, or anything else. As the proverb says, you can "go fast." But because you're a solopreneur or small enterprise, you're also constrained in the volume of things you can do. As a solopreneur, you can't be a full-time marketer, a full-time financier, and a full-time producer. As a small enterprise with a limited staff for each discipline, you eventually bump up against the limits of what your team can produce. To go farther, as the proverb says, "you must go together."

One of the most effective ways an organization can "go farther" is to "go together" with another firm in a Strategic Alliance. Strategic alliances allow firms with complementary product or service offerings to band together to offer their combined services to their respective clients. Strategic alliances are just that, alliances. Neither party takes a financial stake in the other entity. Strategic alliances allow participants to "put their toe in the water" with new offerings without investing in additional training or personnel.

In this week's exercise, I want you to identify some potential strategic alliance partners. Before we jump in, I want to give you one important requirement for making a strategic alliance work. Strategic alliance partners must share core values. Core values are the measuring tool by which you should judge all associations—employees, customers, vendors, *and* strategic alliance partners.

Do this week's exercise on your own or get your leadership team together to answer these questions. Let's jump in.

- **What businesses share the same target audience?** My company has done several strategic alliances, all with partners who serve small-to-medium-sized businesses. I've partnered with other consultants who focus on other disciplines. My focus is strategy and operations. I've done strategic alliances with an HR consultant and a branding consultant. I've done a strategic alliance with a CPA. I've done strategic alliances with two software companies. In each case, customers need the services of both entities, but the service offerings don't overlap. What other companies service the same customers that you service?

- **What businesses are in adjacent spaces?** If you're a roofer, forge a strategic alliance with someone who does gutters. If you're an exterminator, forge a strategic alliance with someone who does wildlife removal.

- **What businesses are further up or further down the value-creation chain?** If you're a restaurant, can you form a strategic alliance with a local farmer to create a special menu item featuring a locally raised or grown product? If you're a restaurant, you might already have forged a strategic alliance with a delivery service like DoorDash that can take prepared meals from your restaurant to the patron's home.

- **If you're in an industry that relies on consumer's discretionary spending, what businesses compete for the same discretionary dollars?** If you're a restaurant, can you partner with a movie theater, axe throwing venue, mini-golf course, or escape room for a complete "night out" package? If you're a florist, can you partner with an event space or caterer to serve those planning a wedding?

- **In a slightly different twist on the strategic alliance, what very similar business serves a different geography?** If you're a garage door repair company in Denver, can you form a strategic alliance with a garage door repair company in Nashville? You could share website development costs, only needing to change logos, contact info, and testimonials. You could share marketing materials.

After you've created your list of potential strategic alliance partners, start making some phone calls. Set up an initial meeting. Start slow. In your initial conversations, you're probing first for shared values. If the potential partner doesn't share your commitment to fair pricing, customer service, and employee development (these are just examples; swap in your nonnegotiable core values), move on to the next potential partner. When you find a good candidate for a strategic alliance, tee up the idea and get a response.

To borrow from Stephen Covey, before you start any strategic alliance, "begin with the end in mind." Define the criteria by which you will judge the success of the alliance. How will you dissolve the alliance if it doesn't produce the results that you had hoped? What will be the disposition of any intellectual property that was created or has been shared during the alliance? What will be the disposition of any new customers gained during the alliance? Conversely, what will the course of action be if the strategic alliance produces stellar results? Will you be free to add that expertise to your own organization in the form of new team members? Will you acquire the other organization, or will your organization be acquired? If you decide to dissolve the alliance, what will be the disposition of new or shared intellectual property? What will be the disposition of any new customers added?

Consider not only the end of the alliance but also the operational details during the alliance. How will revenue be split? Work hard to make the alliance a win-win for both partners. How will each entity promote the new offerings, under their own banner or as an additional offering from a trusted strategic partner? Who will pay for promotion? The more of these questions you answer in advance, the greater the possibility the strategic alliance is a positive experience for both partners.

WEEK 49 :: LEADERSHIP :: NEW SUPERVISORS

Some of the most important work in your company is the work that happens on the front line—when your team members interact with customers. That work drives lifetime customer value, the total revenue available from a customer over the course of their relationship with your company, plus the referrals they provide. Many times, you entrust that work to the lowest-paid person in your company. Someone with the least amount of experience, the least amount of training, and sometimes, the fewest problem-solving skills.

That's what makes your frontline supervisors so important. They schedule, train, and manage these key players in creating value for your customers. Many times, these are folks who have been promoted to supervise their former frontline coworkers. They've distinguished themselves by selling more, building greater rapport with customers, and/or solving problems better than their peers.

This week's One-Year, Thirty-Minute Business Transformation is devoted to crafting a framework that will maximize their effectiveness in their first supervisory role. If your company is committed to promoting from within, this is the feeder system for your future leadership team.

I want you to craft a plan that equips your newly minted supervisor for success. It needs to strike the right balance between developing supervisory skills and mastering new operational details required for their increased responsibilities.

For this week's exercise, I'd grab the people to whom your frontline supervisors report. Depending on the size of your organization, those could be your executive team, or they could be lower-level managers. Spend the thirty-minute exercise focusing on three essential skills for new supervisors—personal growth, position mastery, and employee development.

Personal Growth. It might seem a bit daunting after being promoted to their first supervisory role, but lead the new supervisor to, as Stephen Covey reminded us, "begin with the end in mind." Here are some questions to answer (in no particular order).

- What will the exit from this supervisory role look like? What is the typical career path next step for someone in this supervisory position?

- What skills will the new supervisor need to access those future opportunities?

- How will their supervisor help them transition into this new position, hone the skills needed for the position, and build skills for future positions?

- How will their performance be measured in this position?

- How will the new supervisor identify and develop candidates that will ultimately become their replacement?

- What existing skills can they leverage and grow?

- What existing weaknesses can they shore up?

- How can they get sufficient knowledge in areas in which they are deficient—maybe not resulting in mastery, but at least in becoming "BS-proof"?

- If your organization has an employee development program (which I believe every organization should), much of this should be included there. The week twenty-three One-Year, Thirty-Minute Business Transformation is devoted to employee development programs. However, the development of new supervisors deserves special attention in the organization.

Position Mastery. If there's one activity that consumes a frontline supervisor, it's problem-solving. So equipping them to become better problem solvers automatically makes them better at their job and more valuable to the organization. Effective problem-solving involves empathy, knowledge, creativity, and authority.

- Give your new supervisors policies that empower them. Frontline employees without the authority to solve problems frustrate customers. Supervisors without the authority to solve problems frustrate them even more. If you don't give your employees and supervisors the ability to solve problems, the problems are going to land on your desk. If that's happening, what exactly are you paying those employees for? Good policies are like guardrails on a highway. Your employees are on safe ground using their creativity to solve problems as long as the solution is anywhere between the guardrails.

- Give your new supervisor principles that keep them focused on the outcomes you want. What does the ideal customer experience look like? How can they engineer a resolution that delivers that outcome? What communication would be consistent with the company's brand promise? How can the resolution of a problem help execute the company's mission? How can the resolution of a problem help the organization reach their vision?

- Help your new supervisor gain a bigger perspective. Frontline employees almost exclusively work "in the business." An employee's first supervisory role might represent their first opportunity to work "on the business" albeit in a very limited way. Help them tie their new supervisory responsibilities to bigger ideas like lifetime customer value, employee development, teamwork, organizational health, and value creation. Some employees will "get it" immediately. For others, you might have to connect the dots. For example, explain how taking an extra five minutes to email a customer a summary of the steps you took to replace their faulty but technically out-of-warranty widget will result in boosting their lifetime customer value because the customer will be more likely to purchase from you in the future. Then encourage the supervisor to do similar things with their new direct reports.

Employee Development. For some of your new supervisors, they'll be "boss" to the people with whom they used to work shoulder to shoulder. Some of those people might have been up for the same position and were passed over. And those passed over might still be convinced they were the most deserving candidate. It's a transition that a lot of new supervisors struggle with. There's not a magic bullet that causes the disappointments to subside and harmony to magically return, but some sage advice from Zig Ziglar applies here: "You can have everything in life you want, if you will just help other people get what they want." Instead of turning their attention to "bossing," I'd suggest the new supervisor turn their attention to employee development. Early and often, they should demonstrate their commitment to growing that staff and you should help them do it.

- If your company has a formal employee development plan, get the new supervisor up to speed on how to utilize it as a supervisor; they should already understand how it works as a subordinate. Have them review the already-in-place plans for the staff they are now supervising. If your company does not have an employee development plan, work with the new supervisor to create a framework the supervisor can use to document the goals of their subordinates, the milestones to reach those goals (with time-frames), and the steps to reach those milestones.

- By your example and by specific instruction, show the new supervisor how to explain the "why" behind company policies. Employees who understand the "why" make better decisions and talk more intelligently with customers than those who repeat policies by rote with no understanding of the underlying reasoning. Let the supervisor know it takes longer but returns outsized rewards.

- Help the new supervisor build a unified team with a solid operational framework. Tools like 4DX, OKRs, EOS or my Business Framework get teams aligned, pulling together, and tied to overarching company initiatives.

Of all the things that go on inside an organization, very few, if any, are more important than employee development. And very few employees have a more pivotal role in value creation than frontline supervisors.

As you work through this week's exercise, identify the activities that are most applicable in your organization. You might end up with a couple of variations based on the departments or divisions where the new supervisors are working. Then, work to flesh out the framework with tools, checklists, and activities.

WEEK 50 :: STRATEGIC PLANNING :: INDUSTRY LIFE CYCLE

The Industry Life Cycle concept has been around for decades. It traces the progression of an industry through four stages—introduction, growth, maturity, and decline—each with unique characteristics and implications for the companies in that industry. I've found it attributed to several different business thinkers, so I can't give you the exact originator, but I can tell you it's important and is the topic of this week's One-Year, Thirty-Minute Business Transformation.

Industry Life Cycle differs from Product Life Cycle. Product life cycle traces the progression of a particular product through (depending on what you're reading) four or five stages—development (the fifth that is sometimes added), introduction, growth, maturity (or saturation), and decline. Let's illustrate the difference.

If we were to trace the industry life cycle of home video entertainment in the US, the introduction stage would commence with television and broadcast TV programming in the late 1940s; nine percent of households had a TV in 1950. The growth stage would progress through the 1950s and probably transition to the maturity stage in the late 1950s; eighty-five percent of households had a TV in 1960. Household penetration hit almost 99 percent by 2009. At this point, I'm not sure I can predict a future time when home video entertainment will move into the decline stage. Perhaps that will happen if people shift the bulk of their viewing to personal, portable screens. During this industry life cycle, we've seen dozens of home video-related products move through their own individual product life cycle: black and white tube TVs, color tube TVs, cable programming, satellite, laser discs, VCRs, DVD players, flat screen plasma TVs, and more have yielded to the current crop of OLED TVs, Blu-ray players, streaming boxes, and streaming services (each of which is in its own place in the product life cycle).

What does this have to do with you? It's critical that each person reading this week's post determine where their industry is in the industry life cycle. Each stage dictates specific action and specific investment. I spent the formative years of my business life in a declining industry. They turned "whistling while you walk through the graveyard" into an art form, ignoring the signs that would signal upcoming losses in market share, revenue, and profitability. Any corrections were too little and too late. I left the industry fourteen years ago, but the final trajectory was already apparent.

Let's jump into this week's exercise. If there's ever been a One-Year, Thirty-Minute Business Transformation that requires you to "confront the brutal facts," this is it. If you do this exercise alone, be honest with yourself. If you do this with other team members, there can't be any reprisals for those who express opinions that make you or other coworkers uncomfortable. This is the time for, as Ray Dalio would say in *Principles*, "radical truth and radical transparency."

Let's define the four stages of the industry life cycle and the implications for each industry member in that stage.

Introduction. The products ushering in a new industry are often the creation of a new company. Not only are the products new, but the purveyors of the product might have nonexistent or immature processes, less than foolproof manufacturing, and unsophisticated marketing. Investment priorities for those launching in a new industry include research and development, talent acquisition (plugging talent holes not represented in the launch team), and marketing. And not just any marketing but marketing that resonates with "early adopters," those people who most likely share a passion for the field (food, tech, pets, health, etc.). Their passion supersedes their need for a "perfect" product. Instead, they see the promise of the new industry and want to be pioneers along with the purveyor of the product. If they believe the product has promise, they become advocates for the industry in general and for the purveyor of the product in particular.

Growth. When it's clear that early products have legs, you're here. Customers who buy early in this stage take their cue from the early adopters in the previous stage. Once the early adopters kick the tires and explain the value of the products to those they influence, sales to the "early majority" begin. These are enthusiastic buyers who want to be first to enjoy the benefits of new, proven products. Investment priorities for industry participants at this stage include efficiently scaling up production (driving unit costs down and volume up), building a robust distribution network, and marketing to broader audiences who've shown interest in the industry. Larger "fast followers" from adjacent industries might enter the market via product development or acquisition. As the products constituting the industry become more mainstream and prices go down, the late majority purchase the products, deeming them "safe" and not a fad.

Maturity. At this point, the products constituting the industry have saturated the market. Everyone has one. A shakeout occurs. Producers merge, and most times, better producers gobble up lesser ones. Unit prices continue down, and products become commodities. Investment priorities include acquisitions, efficiency, and, most importantly (while you're flush with cash and if it hasn't surfaced already), looking for the successor product that will perpetuate and strengthen the industry (for example, flip phone to smartphone).

Decline. The products constituting the industry reach the end of their useful life. It becomes apparent that another industry will ultimately consume the same dollars (horse-drawn carriages vs. automobiles). Successor products are now preferred by at least the early adopters and early majority. Sales continue to fall with no chance for recovery. Assets used to produce the product might become worthless if they are useful only for producing that product. Industry members must choose an exit methodology. Depending on the velocity of the decline, one of those can be "the last man standing," but clearly that has a limited lifespan. Ideally participants would have already moved on to other industries and disposed of any specialized assets.

With this backdrop, look critically at your industry. Do your activities and investments mirror the right actions for where you are in the industry life cycle? If the industry is in the growth or maturity stages, are you managing individual product life cycles—creating, promoting, and retiring products— so that you always have the product(s) that deliver(s) optimum value for your customers and target customers?

If you don't engage in continually reinventing your value-creation activities, current and potential competitors will, seeking to capture the money you're making now. This part of the exercise is so important it got its own One-Year, Thirty-Minute Business Transformation earlier this year. You can read about creative destruction in week thirty-four.

The real deliverable from this week's exercise is a set of actions to take into your next strategic planning workshop. You might intensify your R&D activities, reorder your financial priorities, consider your first venture into mergers or acquisitions, focus more attention on operational efficiencies, or contemplate important shifts in messaging, all driven by where you are in the industry life cycle.

WEEK 51 :: GOVERNANCE :: EXECUTION FRAMEWORK

Over the course of the One-Year, Thirty-Minute Business Transformation, we've talked about dozens of responsibilities that fall to you as a leader in your organization, but there's a common thread that weaves its way through all of them. You've got to "get stuff done." Every company I work with has its own unique challenges with getting stuff done. In every case, there's never a shortage of inspiration, good ideas, and plans, but the organization fails, in varying degrees, in execution.

Your company will never carry out its mission or move closer to its vision without a robust Execution Framework. There are already excellent execution frameworks out there. I like OKR (Objectives and Key Results), 4DX (Four Disciplines of Execution), and EOS (Entrepreneur Operating System). I also have my own that's part of my Business Framework. In this week's One-Year, Thirty-Minute Business Transformation, I don't want to advocate for one of these and ask you to select it by the end of the exercise. Instead, I want to communicate the essential elements of an execution framework, explain why they're necessary, and ask you to assess your organization. Identify (1) where your organization is most deficient in execution disciplines, (2) how that deficiency impacts your ability to get stuff done, and (3) what changes need to be made in the organization to correct the deficiency. With that knowledge, you'll be able to select the execution framework that's best suited for your company.

Here are the crucial elements in an execution framework:

- **It makes you connect the dots between the task to be executed and "bigger ideas" in the company—the mission, vision, or an important strategic objective.** If the task doesn't roll up to one of those, why do it?

- **It enforces "cascading."** A big strategic objective involves everyone in the company. Those people work in multiple departments and have very disparate responsibilities. A robust execution framework will allow you to create tasks and subtasks, all rolling up to the big strategic objective.

- **It creates staff alignment.** Everyone in the organization will be able to see how their task traces back to the big strategic objective and how their task complements and enables others in the organization to execute their tasks. Competition and conflict may not be eliminated, but they become subservient to the overarching objective.

- **It pivots on a Responsible Person.** Each task (and cascading subtask) is ultimately "owned" by someone. That person is the sole possessor of the "The buck stops here" sign for that task. As the responsible person, they bear the weight of coordinating the people, resources, and time to bring their particular task to a successful completion.

- **It has mechanisms that create accountability.** As former IBM CEO Louis Gerstner reminded us, "People don't do what you expect, but what you inspect." Depending on the framework, you'll see daily check-in meetings, weekly written reports, intranet dashboards, and several other tools that give responsible parties the opportunity to check progress, learn about emerging roadblocks, and congratulate success.

- **It promotes transparency and communication.** The larger the organization, the more important this becomes. When each team member in the organization can see what the other team members are working on, the opportunity to collaborate (and to reduce redundant work) increases dramatically. Team members can also share what they've discovered during the course of the initiative. This can flatten the learning curve for the organization at large.

- **It provides focus.** The biggest detriment to getting *important* stuff (activities that build long-term organizational health) done is the press of *urgent* stuff (regular, daily tasks that scream for attention right now). The unhappy customer, underperforming vendor, or disgruntled employee provide plenty of distractions. With its ever-present accountability, a good execution framework redirects team members back to "important" tasks as quickly as possible.

- **It tracks resources.** Not only does the framework give visibility into the work of other team members, but it also makes the resources produced by those team members available to everyone else. If a new dataset is created from customer purchase transactions, a new software tool is obtained, or a piece of equipment is purchased, that can be reported on the framework, so it can be leveraged across the organization.

- **It forces prioritization.** No matter how dedicated, talented, and brilliant we might think we are, we can't do more than one or two big strategic initiatives at a time. The discipline required to flesh out an initiative with this degree of detail and push it down through the organization makes you choose just the one or two things that will have the biggest impact on the organization.

- **It utilizes timelines and milestones.** We all know how to eat an elephant: one bite at a time. A good execution framework will help you track tasks as you break them into doable, measurable, and time-appropriate chunks.

- **It makes you pinpoint the right magnitude.** Jim Collins introduced us to "BHAGs"—Big, Hairy, Audacious Goals. Goals that, if you reached them, would make you feel proud and accomplished. Equally, looking at them before the work starts, they are scary. You're not sure you can pull them off. The one or two initiatives in play in your execution framework and the subsequent breakdown of those initiatives into tasks and subtasks ought to cause you some discomfort. If they generate a couple of sleepless nights and a bit of indigestion, you've probably settled in on the right magnitude. If they're a slam dunk, neither you nor your organization are going to grow. If they're too hard, you and your team will get discouraged and give up. Make sure the metrics you use to gauge your success make you stretch to the limit without breaking. The discipline of using a robust framework that requires you to break initiatives into subtasks, assign those tasks to people, and marshal the resources to make the initiatives happen will help you right-size each ability-stretching piece.

- **It's user-friendly.** To maximize its effectiveness, the execution framework must be easy to understand, easy to operate, and easy to access. There should be simple dashboards that show the status of overarching initiatives and drill downs that show progress on subtasks and team member's personal performances. If it's a hassle to enter information or consume information, it will quickly fall into disuse.

I'm guessing it's obvious at this point that the homework for this week's exercise will push you past thirty minutes, but I'm not feeling that sorry. The benefit from finding and implementing the right execution framework for your business will far exceed the investment of extra time. If you're ready to dig deeper, these links will get you more info on the execution frameworks I mentioned earlier.

OKR: https://www.amazon.com/ Measure-What-Matters-Google-Foundation/dp/0525536221/

4DX: https://www.amazon.com/ Disciplines-Execution-Achieving-Wildly-Important/dp/1451627068/

EOS: https://www.amazon.com/Traction-Get-Grip-Your-Business/ dp/1936661837/

Business Framework (see the seventh discipline): https://clearvision.con-sulting/wp-content/uploads/2020/12/BusinessFrameworkOutline.pdf

WEEK 52 :: STRATEGIC PLANNING :: COMPETITIVE LANDSCAPE

In an earlier One-Year, Thirty-Minute Business Transformation, I encouraged you to survey your industry landscape using Porter's Five Forces plus one more (you can read that in week forty-two). It's a valuable exercise because it requires you to zoom out and look at the environment in which you compete from ten thousand feet. For this week's One-Year, Thirty-Minute Business Transformation, you're again going to survey the environment in which you compete, but this time, it won't be from ten thousand feet. Instead, you'll be in the trenches looking at specific competitors, vendors, and distributors with specific actions in mind.

This differs from other exercises where the endgame was evolutionary: changes in the attitudes and actions of leadership, a change in processes, or a change in a specific discipline in the organization. The changes emerging from this exercise can be revolutionary. Executed well, they can return 3x, 5x, or 10x growth. Executed poorly, they can decimate the organization's reputation and finances. In other words, big risk and big rewards.

Let's jump in.

- **Identify competitors that you admire.** They might be local, regional, national, or online. Why do you admire them? Do they have a fanatical customer base that keeps buying and singing their praises while they do it? Do they have robust processes for delivering their products and services? Is their messaging engaging? Do they have a readily recognizable brand? Do they have a uniquely talented staff that is driving their organization ahead?

- **With that competitor in mind:**

  - **Can you emulate any of the things you admire?** Strategists discuss "absorptive capacity"—the ability to observe the value drivers in a competitor's product or delivery, internalize them, remake them (taking into account your company's unique personality), and redeploy them to eradicate the other company's advantage. Is this a possibility for any of the things you admire in your competitors? Keep in mind, if you do this, it must make economic sense, and any imitation must still be consistent with your brand, values, and culture.

  - **Would it make any sense to pursue a merger or acquisition?** You never know what might be going on inside that organization. You might have an owner eager to sell their company or one that's looking to acquire a company like yours. Horizontal integration immediately increases market share (by eliminating a competitor and capturing their customers as your own) and cuts unit costs (by spreading fixed costs over more sales volume). Typically in a merger or acquisition, the new enterprise eliminates redundancy (you don't need two finance departments, two HR departments, etc.) while retaining newly acquired product or service offerings. Be warned, however: integrating two organizations is extremely difficult. It must be done well to realize the full financial benefit of the merger or acquisition. Read more about mergers and acquisitions in week twenty-two.

  - **Would it make any sense to pursue a strategic alliance or joint venture?** Collaboration among competitors can make sense when each one has unique products, delivery methodologies, or competencies from which the other could benefit. You can offer your customers additional products or services (originating from the competitor) and still keep them in the fold. Your strategic alliance partner can offer their customers products and services provided by you. Additionally, both of you can learn from the other. Neither party is likely to expose or unfairly leverage newly learned trade secrets since the other party could do likewise in retaliation. Read more about alliances in week forty-eight.

- **Are there any suppliers that it might make sense to acquire?**
Moving upstream in the value-creation chain sometimes makes sense. Could you more effectively create value for customers if you had complete control over a particular supplier? Could you benefit from the additional margin now taken by the supplier, or could you benefit from prioritizing your own delivery of their product or service? While these are certainly two benefits you could derive from acquiring an upstream supplier, there are plenty of potential downsides to consider:

  - Do you have sufficient knowledge to operate in that industry?

  - Are you comfortable selling to your competitors? It's unlikely that you consume all of the product coming from that supplier. The supplier probably sells to your competitors also.

  - If you were to buy the company, are your competitors OK with buying from you?

  - If a new technology emerges that makes the products you purchase from that supplier available at a greatly reduced price, you can easily switch to the new, cheaper supplier. However, if you've purchased that current supplier, then the new technology emerges, you're stuck with a company whose customer base is fleeing to the new, cheaper supplier. Depending on the circumstances, you might also be stuck using your own more expensive supply while your competitors cut their cost of goods sold. Plus, you might be stuck with a company whose value is plummeting as their product falls out of favor with the market.

- **Are there any distributors that it might make sense to acquire?** Moving downstream in the value-creation chain can make sense also. It gets you closer to the customer and allows you to capture the margin now going to the downstream distributor. This interaction with downstream parties can help you become more innovative as you more intimately understand problems that you can solve with new products and delivery mechanisms. You might up your "creative destruction" game significantly. You also have the ability to exercise more control over the customer's experience with your product or service. However, just like moving upstream, moving downstream has some risk. More interaction requires more resources—people, communication infrastructure, and customer-facing tech just to name a few.

Many of the One-Year, Minute Business Transformations have much shorter runways and yield their fruit quickly, some in mere days or weeks. This one is decidedly different. You won't see the full financial impact of these initiatives for years. Confer with trusted advisers and make haste slowly. If you forge ahead with one or more of these, do it well. Get help if you need to. Stakes are high, screwups are expensive, but rewards are huge.

NOW WHAT?

If you've made it to here, thank you. I hope you're reaping plenty of benefits from the work you've done already—and make no mistake, this is work. Kudos go to you and your team for tackling the essential task of improving organizational health.

But what do you do now that you've completed all the exercises?

As you know, the exercises were very different.

- Some installed a new practice in your organization (like *Employee Development* or *Customer Onboarding*). You've got to keep those practices going and you've got to circle back periodically to see if they need a facelift. Continuous improvement is proof that you're committed to another exercise—*Learning Orientation*.

- Some called for a gut check (like *Confront the Brutal Facts* or *On the Business vs. In the Business*). I hope those will hang on in your head and heart and become part of your leadership DNA. And I hope you'll pass those along to your leadership team as part of the culture you're building.

- Some encouraged you to make your team better, smarter, and more valuable to the organization (like *Financial Literacy* and *Hard Skills and Soft Skills*). The question always surfaces, "Am I just preparing my employees for their next employer?" Maybe. But creating employees that everyone wants to hire is a pretty good legacy and a big compliment to you and your team. And yet-to-be-hired employees will want to work for you because they know your company is a place where they can learn skills that will serve them well their entire career. One piece of encouragement from Richard Branson: "Train people well enough so they can leave; treat them well enough so they don't want to."

- Some were like tuning up your car—something you need to do, not every day but periodically, to keep things running smoothly (like *Staying Even, Getting Ahead* and *Evaluating Tech Productivity*). Determine the right frequency for updating these disciplines in your organization and get the "tune up" on your calendar.

- There might even be some that you've invited into other areas of your life. Certainly the chapter on *Personal Growth* was meant for that, but maybe you found other uses for the principles from *Decision Making* and *Change.*

The One-Year, Thirty-Minute Business Transformation is all about incremental change—which is a good thing. But I hope that the changes you saw in yourself, your team, and your organization whetted your appetite for a bigger bite out of the apple. That's one reason the exercise on *Annual Plan* was included in the book. It encouraged you to put together the pieces for an annual strategic planning exercise. I hope you'll do it. If you engage in a good strategic planning exercise, you'll include a lot of the "tune up" topics, and you'll engage your team in important "gut check" conversations all within the context of the new practices that are now an integral part of your organization.

There's something about taking three or four days away from the crush of daily activities and talking solely (and truthfully) about "where we are now, where we want to be, and how we're going to get from the former to the latter" that changes an organization. If you and your team do it well, you'll come back unified and with incredible clarity that can translate into large-scale, trajectory-altering transformation for your organization. But one word of warning: the best strategic plans in the world are worthless without diligent execution. Incorporate one of the frameworks from the *Execution Framework* exercise to roll out the plan in your organization.

Notwithstanding, strategic planning exercise or no strategic planning exercise, you now have a lot of good tools in your toolbox. Pull specific tools out as frequently as you need them. My guess is that something like *Environment for Growth* might get used almost daily while *Mergers and Acquisitions* might not get used but once every few months. That's OK. The important thing is that you circle back to each of these tools as often as is necessary to keep your organization healthy.

You're doing something important. Your family, your team members, and the families of your team members are reaping the benefits of your good work. You're making the lives of your customers better and you're strengthening your community.

And you're not alone. You're part of the One-Year, Thirty-Minute Business Transformation community. You can interact with them on the forum on the book website, oneyearthirtyminute.com.

And like I said in the very beginning of the book, I'm cheering you on. If I can be a resource for you, contact me at mchirveno@clearvision.consulting.

Thank you.

ACKNOWLEDGEMENTS

I'm pretty sure that since I began consulting in 2006, I've learned more from my clients and their teams than they've learned from me. Their challenges have made me dig deep and create a lot of what you just read. Their successes are filed away in my "bag of tricks." Those are represented in the book too. Their businesses have been the laboratory where these ideas were tested and honed. I've made lifelong friends.

Teaching at Baker University has been a wonderful experience. I've had the privilege of working with smart, dedicated adult learners. They've forced me to think differently and find better ways to communicate the information in this book.

People I only know through their written words have had an oversized influence in this book. My bookshelves and Kindle are full of books from Jim Collins, Clayton Christensen, Patrick Lencioni, Dan Pink, Ryan Holiday, Charles Koch, Donald Miller, Seth Godin, Bernadette Jiwa, John Doerr, Cal Newport, Jonah Berger, Rich Karlgaard, Marcus Buckingham, Eric Schmidt, Gary Keller, Stephen Covey, David Flint, Ray Dalio, Annie Duke, and many more. They have challenged and stretched my strategic and operational thinking. I've synthesized their ideas with, hopefully, some original ideas forged in the crucible of good work with clients. I think most writing is a mashup of the books we've read, the people we've met, the experiences we've had, and a lot of mental meandering. That's certainly the case here.

I'd be remiss if I didn't recognize the mother of all educations—twenty-four years in the publishing industry with lots of fine folks at the *Kansas City*

Star. If there's an operations job I didn't have or a type of project I didn't manage, I don't know what it is. And my bosses were willing to let me figure them all out and make them all happen even though I didn't have a formal education in many of those disciplines. Special shoutouts to Jeff Hall who led with passion and demanded excellence; Bob Woodworth, the best question-asker ever; Wes Turner who frequently quoted Lou Gerstner for me, "People don't do what you expect; they do what you inspect"; Mark Contreras who enthusiastically advocated for my work; and Lisa Parks who always encouraged me to autograph my work with excellence.

Most of the words in this book were penned (technically they were typed) at Messenger Coffee in downtown Kansas City, MO. The sun beaming through the giant windows, the aroma from coffee and freshly baked goodies, business meetings taking place at several tables in the café, and, most of all, the staff who deliver "function, form, and feeling" (see chapter 11) provided the perfect backdrop for writing. Messenger Coffee is not a client, and I've never met the ownership group, but the business wonderfully illustrates several of the themes in the book (healthy culture, learning orientation, and valuable strategic partners). When someone who does what I do for a living sees a business making it work, it's like a shot of adrenaline—a bit of encouragement to work hard for the next client, so they too can build the business they've always dreamed about.

My friends and spiritual family at New Life CityChurch have been a source of encouragement, strength, and wise counsel. When life feels like the Old Testament book of Job, their support has been like chapters thirty-eight through forty-two, not chapters four through thirty-seven. Special shoutout to Troy Campbell who helped me through one of the darkest times in my life.

You don't leave a steady paycheck and do your own thing without a supportive family. My wife Leslie, daughter Liz, and son Nick are the best nuclear family anyone could ever have. Their love and support is constant and unwavering. A special shoutout to my mom, Betty, who, along with my wife, insisted that this book get done sooner rather than later.

INDEX

CPSIA information can be obtained
at www.ICGtesting.com
Printed in the USA
BVHW061321171121
621781BV00011B/694